GERVASUTTI'S CLIMBS

Publisher's Note

The name Giusto Gervasutti is not widely known in America except to a few real aficianados of climbing literature, and indeed an English version of Gervasutti's autobiography was not translated from Italian until 1957, eleven years after his untimely death. However, in Europe he is known as one of the outstanding climbers of his generation. The Mountaineers take pleasure in making this book available to readers on this continent who will want to learn about his significant climbing record as well as share introspection into the motivation behind his accomplishments.

Other mountain classics reprinted by The Mountaineers include *Tales of a Western Mountaineer*, *The Ascent of Denali*, *Unknown Mountain*, *Across the Olympic Mountains* and *Challenge of the North Cascades*. The publishers plan to continue to make such historic books more widely available. Please address suggestions for future reprints to The Mountaineers (Books), 719 Pike Street, Seattle, WA 98101.

Giusto Gervasutti

GIUSTO GERVASUTTI

Gervasutti's Climbs

translated by
NEA MORIN
and
JANET ADAM SMITH

THE MOUNTAINEERS
SEATTLE

THE MOUNTAINEERS... Organized 1906
"... to explore, study, preserve and enjoy
the natural beauty of Northwest America ... "

Published simultaneously in Great Britain
by Diadem Books Ltd.,
85 Ballards Lane, London N.3

Printed in Great Britain
by Billing & Sons Limited

Library of Congress No. 87-70839
ISBN No. 0-916890-67-8

Contents

Ten : 1938

Eleven : 1939 to 1942

Twelve : Conclusion

GLOSSARY

Illustrations

FOREWORD

By Lucien Devies

Giusto Gervasutti was killed in September 1946, attempting a new climb on Mont Blanc du Tacul. In August of that year he had made the second ascent of a route on the mountain which had first been done in 1936 by Gabriele Boccalatte and Nini Pietrasanta. On this climb he had been fascinated by the great sweep of the central pillar immediately to the left of the lower half of the Boccalatte route and recognised the possibility of a new climb of great technical interest and difficulty—though in his view the Boccalatte route would always remain the logical line of ascent.

In the second week of September the weather improved and he set out with Gagliardone, who had been his partner on the north face of the Grandes Jorasses. At eight o'clock on September 16, with Giusto in great form, the two started up the rocks of the central pillar. Almost straightaway they were confronted by two exceedingly difficult pitches, on each of which they used four pitons. After negotiating some short steep walls they took a line up the left flank of the pillar; again, the climbing was extremely difficult. At 3.20 they were nearly half-way up the face, but there were signs of a break in the weather. So, as conditions were bad on the upper part of the face anyway, they decided to turn back. After climbing down for a couple of rope-lengths, they tied their two ropes together for a ninety-foot rappel down a pitch with an overhang at the top. Then, after trying in vain to pull the ropes down after them, they decided to climb up again. Leaving their sacks on a small ledge they tied themselves on to the two ends of the combined rope—Gagliardone to the end of the shorter one, Gervasutti to the longer. Half-way up the slabs to the overhang Gervasutti put in a piton and brought Gagliardone up so that the latter could belay him for the next move. Having recovered enough

9

rope, Gervasutti climbed up over the overhang, and called
out that the ropes wouldn't run because the knot joining them
had stuck in a crack. Gagliardone then went down again to
the ledge, and Giusto called out to him to unrope quickly, and
get all the pitons out of the sack so that they could rope down
at top speed in order to avoid a bivouac. While Gagliardone
was doing this he heard a fall and an anguished cry, and as he
looked up he saw Giusto hurtling down the slabs on his left
about ten or twelve feet away, with the shorter of the two ropes
still running through the rappel loop. Giusto must have fallen
in the act of taking hold of the rappel. Somehow, instead of
getting his hand on both ropes he must have gripped only one
—the longer of the two—which he dragged down with him.

Gagliardone saw him fall practically the whole way down the
face. He was utterly stunned. But he managed to pull himself
together and, although alone and without a rope, he faced up
to the situation with remarkable courage. Somehow, with a
tremendous effort, he succeeded in getting down about 800 feet.
Then, at 7.30 (the fall had occurred about 5), he saw a party
returning from the Aiguille du Midi and called for help: the
guides promised to come as soon as it was light next morning.
Gagliardone bivouacked barely three hundred feet above the
place where Giusto lay, and when the rescue party arrived at
the wall next morning they had no difficulty in finding the
body. E. Bron, A. Gobbi, and L. Grivel climbed the couloir
beside the pillar to a point level with Gagliardone and thirty
feet away, from which they threw him a rope. He climbed over
to them, and by early afternoon they were down on the glacier.

Such was the end of the greatest Italian mountaineer, indeed
one of the greatest mountaineers of all time, with whose name
are associated some of the finest expeditions of our day.

Giusto Gervasutti was a climber of the very highest class, not
only on account of the brilliance of his actual achievements,
but because of the spirit in which he undertook them. His
physique was superb: his strength was backed by exceptional
endurance, and he trained assiduously. Master of every type
of climbing, and of every technique, he was constantly trying
to improve on his own standard. Everyone who had seen him

in action agreed that he was a born climber of quite exceptional
quality—one of those rare, outstanding figures who emerge from
time to time in every sport. He had a magnificent style, perfect in its simplicity and effectiveness—the style of a conqueror
—and his combination of virtuosity and precision inspired one
with absolute confidence.

In the moral qualities without which no man can become a
great mountaineer he was as richly endowed; cool, equable
and controlled in the most critical situations, quick in decision
and imperturbably brave. Yet there was nothing fanatical in
his approach to climbing; and ready as he was to accept the
strenuous moral challenge which mountains offer, he never
failed to respond also to their poetry. Giusto's characteristic
independence was illustrated in 1937, when officials of the
Italian Alpine Club requested him to break off his climbing
partnership with me on political grounds. Giusto refused
point-blank, saying that he climbed for his own pleasure and
not in the least for national prestige.

Few climbers have identified themselves so completely with
their sport, or been willing to run so many risks. When we
started out for the north-west wall of the Ailefroide, which we
expected to be every bit as hard as the north face of the Grandes
Jorasses, Giusto slipped on the moraine and fractured two ribs.
From his experience after a ski-ing accident, he reckoned that
he would be able to keep going for a day; so, in order not to
miss the climb, we decided to carry on, although he knew that I
was not in good shape myself after a recent attack of appendi-
citis. He climbed magnificently all the first day, but during the
bivouac the cold made the pain much worse. Climbing the
final wall, which was thickly coated with verglas, was a struggle
of the utmost severity, and for Giusto it was an agonising
ordeal, which he came through triumphantly.

Giusto was the perfect companion, and ours was a good
partnership. For all the difference of language and nationality
we understood each other perfectly and our minds worked in
much the same way, both in planning and carrying out a climb.
Our friendship was as bright as ever, and the moment for
which I had been waiting seven years had come at last: we were

about to join forces again, and had various expeditions in mind. It is hard to believe that it is all over. All that remains is the memory of the great things we did together—and they will not easily be forgotten. But I am convinced that if, at the moment of his death, Giusto had a fraction of a second in which to think of himself and his life, he must have died content. Dear Giusto, you always went straight ahead on the way you had discovered and made your own, creating for yourself a life of ever increasing ardour, depth and radiance.

One : Initiation

Cima Grande di Lavaredo—Cima Piccola di Lavaredo—Campanile di Val Montanaia—North wall of Monte Siera—Chamonix—Aiguille Verte—Grépon

I HAVE often wondered how my passion for mountains came into being, but it is rather like trying to remember when one first learnt to swim—somehow one always seems to have known. Nearly always there is one determining factor, whether supplied by chance or of one's own making, which impels a person towards whatever type of activity he chooses. Yet I have never been able to decide what exactly it was that aroused the passion which was so greatly to influence the whole of my life.

I am not sure whether I ought to regret not having joined one of the many groups which were being formed at the time, in particular by the S.U.C.A.I. (Universities' Section of the Italian Alpine Club), or whether I should consider it an advantage that I started on my own. It may well have been a finer experience for me to come to mountaineering gradually, with no fixed ideas or definite intentions, my only motive to please myself. Not until later did I discover that here was a field of action where I could satisfy my need for struggle and adventure.

Mountains—or rather the mountain landscape of the Carnic Alps, where I went every year for the holidays—had from the first made a tremendous impression upon my childish imagination. I was fascinated by the torrent thundering down the gorges, the foaming waterfall hemmed in by steep tree-crowned rocks, the deep mysterious cavern where terrible brigands lurked in days of old. From the crumbling rock above, enormous avalanches crashed down into the valley—the work, so it was said, of the accursed Mascardo toiling night and day to expiate a sin. Higher up, above the pinewoods and the chalets

13

and the sheep pastures, was a region of goblins and fairies, gnomes and elves. How wonderful to a child's imaginative mind was this world where torrent and waterfall took on fantastic proportions, where forest and cave were the setting for marvellous adventures, where, too, the rambling stories told by the old woodcutter round his smoky hearth encouraged even more romantic daydreams.

As the years went by the woods became something more than a setting for my own imaginings. I discovered that the wind murmuring in the leaves and the water roaring in the gorge spoke with voices of their own; when nightfall surprised me alone on the high pastures, strange feelings possessed me, to which I could not give a name. I exulted in new powers; in climbing steep slopes and never tiring; in the effortless ease of my muscles' response. It was no longer the torrent, the waterfall, or the cavern that was all-important; it was through the life of action that I would now realise my dreams, and my wanderings took me up towards the pale or flaming summits that evoked in me such strange desires.

It was edelweiss that led me on to greater things: not the small edelweiss you find on the last patches of grass, but the kind that grows only on steep and apparently inaccessible places, and is far more difficult to gather. And so I discovered another pleasure: climbing rocks. My hands learnt to search out the safest holds, my feet acquired confidence and precision. I roamed from mountain to mountain, eager to see new things, but above all determined to overcome the fear and uneasiness of the valley-dweller. At last came the day when I succeeded in setting foot upon the highest and hardest summit in the district. There, before me, lay a whole new unsuspected world: majestic mountains with great sheer walls, or slender spires on which, so it looked from a distance, only an eagle could set foot. They were the Cadore Dolomites.

Looking on my own mountains, nearly all of them low and rounded, I felt humiliated. Over there, now, one really would have to struggle for one's summit. And so the first step was taken towards that all-powerful desire for heroic but unnecessary action which lies at the heart of mountaineering, and which has always been an essential, though hidden, force at the heart of all man's noblest enterprises, great or small.

In wintertime, at home, I read all I could about mountains. In this way I learned of the existence of a whole world of German mountaineers, whose record was unrivalled—and this at the time was not without political significance—on mountains that were now wholly Italian. I learned also that small groups of Italian climbers, first from Trentino and then from Vicenza and Belluno, were beginning to challenge, and successfully to overcome, difficulties of ever-increasing severity. I heard too of a local guide—a legendary figure in the district—who reigned supreme over those rock spires that were inaccessible to me.

All this had the result of keeping me off climbing instead of bringing me closer. How could I venture alone among these frightening strangers without first having the exact measure of my own strength? At this point, Severino Casara lent me the proofs of a little book entitled *Guide to the Eastern Dolomites* by Professor Berti, which was published the following year by the Venice section of the Italian Alpine Club. In it the difficulties were graded, while a certain measure of mystery and poetry was retained—a rare virtue in a guide-book. I owe a lot to it, for it was this book that really gave direction to my early Alpine activity, and supplied the powerful impulse which led me, inexperienced as I was, to challenge the formidable and unknown difficulties of the Dolomites.

The following summer, with two of the friends who had accompanied me upon my previous wanderings, I ventured on my first real Alpine expedition. Readers may think it odd to find an old-fashioned flavour in this account of things that happened not so long ago. But remember our peculiar situation; we were completely cut off from the main mountaineering centres, and we did not even know how to use a rope! Like our friends, the game-wardens, we were equipped for our excursions with a long iron-spiked staff, with a superb chamois horn at the other end of it, which I still cherish with my other treasures—a mythical sword for slaying imaginary dragons! Our first concern, therefore, was to obtain some suitable equipment; then to draw up our programme with the aid of Berti's guide-book. The nearest mountains, and those which attracted us most, were the Tre Cime di Lavaredo (the Drei Zinnen). Our choice was prompted partly by the boldness of their outline, partly by their Alpine history, and also by the fact that during the first world war they had been the scene of some remarkable exploits. Among the best known are those of Sepp Innerkofler, holder of the Austrian Gold Medal, who had climbed the north face of the Cima Piccola by night in order to direct artillery fire; and of De Luca of the Alpine troops who, after an epic duel, hurled the said Innerkofler together with a large boulder off the crest of the Paterno. The ascent of the Cima Ovest di Lavaredo was to be our first test; the second, the Cima Piccola, a springboard for the greater conquests we so keenly desired (I can remember how enthusiastically I read the descriptions of Preuss's and Dülfer's climbs and of the direttissima on the Civetta). If these ascents were successful, we planned to move on to the Spalti di Toro.

The proud alpenstock was relegated to the hayloft and, equipped with a flamboyant new rope, we made our way up to Misurina at the beginning of July. It rained solidly for four days. On the fourth we were cheered by a glimpse of the sun, and on the morning of the fifth we set out with beating hearts. But all went well. Our long expeditions in the Carnic Alps, with neither ropes nor directions about routes, when we had followed chamois tracks along sloping ledges and up walls of steep grass, had been wonderful training, and the difficulties we had so much feared now vanished into thin air. But we were not able to rest upon our laurels on the summit for long, for the mist, which had surrounded us all day, was followed by a violent storm. On the descent our misfortunes began— they were due to lack of experience. The snow held us up, and in our haste to get down we took to a couloir on the west face. Very soon we were brought up short on the verge of a formidable precipice. We had mistakenly made straight for the exit of the Dülfer route on the west face, a route which at that time had not been repeated! With an eighty-foot rope for the three of us, and with no hammer, pitons or karabiners, the situation was not very funny. With great difficulty we climbed up again, and after a prolonged search found the right route. Night had fallen by the time we had finished the descent and we were in a pretty poor way.

After a rest day we were off again, this time to attack the Piccola. And now our lack of technique began to tell. After various incidents (the traverse we found particularly hard going, as it was still covered with snow from the storm ten days before), we arrived at the shoulder, and stopped to examine the Zsygmondy chimney. We didn't altogether like the look of it, and while we were discussing the best method of tackling it —whether to use a left or right leg when getting out at the top —a young guide, who seemed to float up the rocks, emerged from the last crack beneath us. (We were to find out later that this was Angelo Dimai.) We stood aside, leaving the pitch free for him. He had in tow a German weighing about fifteen stone who succeeded in getting himself completely wedged in the chimney, and nothing could move him. The guide's curses, the client's legs waving madly in the air, the whole enormous bulk incapable of going either up or down, put us in high good humour again and I tackled the pitch. I must confess, however, that it wasn't quite as simple as all that. At the top, under the overhang, I also got jammed too far in. In spite of my fear of hanging out above space I had to make up my mind to it, and with a desperate wriggle of elbows and knees I managed to get out in a rush, contrary to every rule of technique—or so I later discovered.

On the descent we climbed down, for as yet we knew nothing about rappels.

But our confidence grew with these first difficulties. We moved over to the Spalti di Toro, and after two or three moderately interesting climbs we decided to try the Campanile di Val Montanaia. This curious little dolomitic structure, the scene of some dramatic and much discussed exploits, enjoyed at the time a far greater reputation than its real difficulty warranted. This was no doubt due partly to the extreme exposure of the climb itself (there were few climbers then who made use of pitons and karabiners for belays), and also to its isolation, for it was surrounded by a protective circle of higher summits, as if to keep itself from prying eyes.

So for us it was a red-letter day when we reached the top of this peak, and the tinkling of the little bell which climbers from the Venetian Alps had set up there by way of consecration, seemed to us a most happy augury for future conquests. That day on the airy summit, with silence all round and the sun turning the peaks to flame, I understood that mountaineering was to become for me a second form of existence, on a higher plane than the daily life to which we are normally restricted. I longed for other goals in distant lands, still untrodden and unknown, and this longing has never left me.

Another year went by, and the summer saw our party once more assembled. During the winter I had read Mummery's *My Climbs in the Alps and Caucasus*, and I had been especially struck by a paragraph which I quote from his chapter on "The Pleasures and Penalties of Mountaineering". "The true mountaineer is a wanderer, and by a wanderer I do not mean a man who expends his whole time in travelling to and fro in the mountains on the exact tracks of his predecessors—much as a bicyclist rushes along the turnpike roads of England—but I mean a man who loves to be where no human being has been before, who delights in gripping rocks that have previously never felt the touch of human fingers, or in hewing his way up ice-filled gullies whose grim shadows have been sacred to the mists and avalanches since 'Earth rose out of chaos'."

These words made me realise that we could not consider ourselves real mountaineers until we had proved ourselves on some new route. So, filled with our new self-confidence, and after a rigorous training and some difficult climbs, we set out to find a wall that was still virgin. Our choice fell upon one of our old acquaintances in the Carnic Alps: the north face of Monte Siera—a 2,500 foot rock-wall overhanging Sappada. In passing we had already admired this wall, and we knew that the guides and climbers of the district had attempted it without success.

As often happens in mountain districts off the beaten track, a terrible and mysterious reputation had grown up round this wall. The few chamois-hunters to whom we had gone for information about a possible point of attack, looked at us pityingly. They did everything in their power to terrify us by describing the smooth slabs and vertical chimneys which made the mountain inaccessible, and the avalanches of whining stones—more hypothetical than real—which poured ceaselessly down in the depths of the couloirs. But we were strong in the knowledge of our conquests in the Dolomites, and ready to tackle anything.

We pitched our tent on the edge of the forest, and then through powerful glasses examined—though without much result—the deep furrows that appeared and disappeared as the sun moved round the mountain. In the afternoon we were visited by a large party of summer visitors from Udine—young men and girls, old school-friends of ours, who had heard of our intentions from the chamois-hunters we had questioned, and who had now come to dissuade us from carrying out our daring plan. "The guides haven't been able to do it, and yet *you* want to?" The girls looked at us with such compassion. Poor boys, they must have thought, so young, and practically bound to be killed by that horrible mountain up there . . . What an idea! But the only result was to make us more obstinate than ever. After all, hadn't we climbed the Piccola Cima with Dimai, and rung the bell on the summit of the Campanile di Val Montanaia? And we now had a hammer, three pitons and a karabiner!

In the evening the party went back to the village, and, unable to sleep, we were left to speculate on what the mountain had in store for us. Next morning, serene and confident, we set forth to the attack. After eight hours' climbing the wall was conquered, for although the difficulties were sustained, they did not exceed grade III. Awaiting us on the summit was an old guide from Sappada. From the ridge he had followed the final stages of the ascent, and he was so moved that he insisted on roping up with us for the descent, leaving me the honour of coming down last.

In the course of another year our field of action gradually widened. I now found a companion and teacher in Stegagno, an engineer, a long-standing member of the S.U.C.A.I., and a great lover of snow and ice climbs. We arranged a short season in the Hohe Tauern together: a first, and very arduous, experience with crampons and ice-axe where, of course, I had everything to learn. But the climbs on our programme were not hard, and on ice the whole secret lies in determination, which one doesn't lack in one's teens. It was these climbs that opened the way for me to the Western Alps.

The following winter I settled in Turin, and my ambitions at once turned towards the high Alps, the birthplace of mountaineering. After long training on spring Sundays among the foothills and valleys of Lanzo, I went with Emilio Lupotto to Chamonix. We stepped off the train at the famous Savoy resort; there was the colourful and elegant crowd of visitors strolling along the middle of the streets, and the celebrated guides, at pains to indoctrinate the clients whom they would later have to haul up the interminable slopes of the Monarch of the Alps. Telescopes were focussed on the great glaciers so that those who dared venture no further than the tennis courts might tremble at the crossing of crevasses, organised (or very nearly) like those in *Tartarin*. We felt rather lost— like country boys arriving for the first time in a big city. We spent most of the rest of the day looking for a hotel to suit our slender purses, and trying to get our bearings so that we could draw up our programme of climbs. After dinner we sauntered out into the streets of Chamonix and stopped in the little square where stands the statue of Balmat and de Saussure. The evening air was clear, almost cold, in the last rays of the setting sun; somewhere, an orchestra was playing a plaintive tune, and such was my state of mind that the music made me feel immediately more sensitive, more receptive than usual. There, before me, for the first time, lay the Mont Blanc massif. At last I too would be able to measure myself against its classic problems, and I too would come to know its oft proclaimed beauties which I had only been able to imagine from the accounts of others.

Mont Blanc is not only the highest mountain in Europe; the

massif as a whole offers, for the greater pleasure of mountaineers, the widest possible variety of climbing. When seen from the valley, or from a long way off, most of the details do not stand out, because the huge bulk of the main mass predominates. So, to the superficial observer, other mountains celebrated in history and tradition (such as the Matterhorn—a rival monarch) may appear more imposing, bolder in conception, conceived and constructed by an architect of superior genius. This is true of a distant view. But on the man who actually climbs them they make a very different impression. On the Matterhorn the bold architectural structure, which one admires so much from below, is broken up into details of lesser aesthetic value—though it still has a savage grandeur—but in the Mont Blanc group closer acquaintance reveals a whole new world previously unseen. And this world waits for the mountaineer who seeks out its different faces in their ever-changing aspects. Here the obelisk of the Drus thrusts up a column of petrified despair; the menacing north face of the Grandes Jorasses rears the pitiless sequence of its slabs above the leaden-hued Mer de Glace. Here are the dizzy Brenva slopes, flanked by the Peuterey ridge—the finest in all the Alps—and, gleaming darkly, like gigantic crystals, the red pillars of the south wall.[1] Pointed Aiguilles soar up on every side, challenging the skies and defying the pygmies who dare to climb them.

On that first visit, what I most enjoyed thinking of was the inspiring struggle for the conquest of the untrodden peak— and, as night came on, I seemed to see Balmat come to life and point out the long, toilsome, hidden route to de Saussure. Jacques Balmat was indeed the first great mountaineer in the full sense of the word as we understand it today. In books, the history of mountaineering usually begins with de Saussure's conquest of Mont Blanc. It is easy to understand how the name of the celebrated and illustrious savant should have come to eclipse that of the rough mountain peasant, but this disparity

---

[1] The first ascent of this route, the Piliers de Fresney, was made by Giusto Gervasutti and Paolo Bollini della Predosa on 13 August 1940 (see Chapter XI). The route lies up one of the great parallel red pillars which decorate the broad face that lies between the Peuterey and Innominata ridges. [Translators' Note.]

of reputation is not borne out by the facts, at any rate so far as actual mountaineering is concerned.

From the time of his first visit to Chamonix, de Saussure realised how valuable it would be for him to reach a height hitherto unattained. He had already discovered a new method of scientific research on the study of natural phenomena, and he needed the endorsement of some major experiments. He returned from an ascent to the summit of the Brévent, a magnificent viewpoint for Mont Blanc, with the conviction that he must climb the mountain; and he announced a substantial reward to the person who should discover a route, and lead him to the top. Science, then—the most noble of motives—was the first consideration. As his writings show quite plainly, de Saussure was open-minded enough to perceive and understand the aesthetic appeal of the mountain, but he lacked the spirit of adventure. The wild, unknown places of the earth, which had always attracted all great explorers, held no appeal for him. He felt no urge to brave the glaciers whose tongues thrust down towards the emerald green pastures, nor yet to lead the mountain peasants who were to search for a route, nor even to encourage them and set an example by sharing the dangers and mysteries of the unknown. He was content to remain at a distance and say: "Go, then come and fetch me, and I will reward you."

Perhaps his contemporary, Bourrit, better deserved to be called the father of mountaineering. He loved the mountains passionately; he was an artist, and struggled to express all that was deepest and most moving in them. To a greater extent, and to better effect than de Saussure, he took part in the early phases of the struggle for the conquest of Mont Blanc. He encouraged the guides, he re-established their morale when they returned worn out and terrified by the new and awful things they had seen on the heights, he persuaded them to try again. He himself took part in some of the attempts, and was the first of those who were not mountain-bred who dared to follow the local men in their efforts. But he lacked ability, for his enthusiasm and faith were not backed up by sufficient physical strength; even more marked was his lack of determination and strength of purpose. For these reasons Bourrit was useless when actually on the mountains. The Chamonix pioneers were men of strength and courage, spurred on not only by the reward promised by de Saussure, but also by a fierce and ever-increasing rivalry.

The struggle between man and mountain continued for over twenty years without appreciable progress being made.

Meanwhile Balmat was growing up. Like his companions in this particular struggle, he too hunted game and searched for crystals. But he was a man of outstanding enterprise and ambition, interested in everything he saw, and this gave him his superiority over the others. He wished to be what he was not and could not be: he wanted to accomplish things new and unknown. Deep in his heart, he cherished in embryonic form, the selfsame hopes and thoughts that were already a clear and conscious reality in both Bourrit's artistic spirit and in de Saussure's comprehensive and imaginative mind. Later Balmat was to prove this, when he set himself to study, in however disorderly a way—gathering stones and plants, not to sell but to keep, like the savants, for his own private collection; plunging into new enterprises, such as that systematic prospecting for mines which was to lead later to his death. He was a man of heroic mould, with the enthusiasm of the indomitable fighter who never gives in; there was an inner force that surged up in him, like a prisoner desperately seeking freedom.

The others told the tales of their attempts, describing the exhausting plods up long snow slopes, the overwhelming blizzards, the unbearable heat in the couloirs, which parched their throats like a desert wind; they reported how the giant Chamonix guide, whose herculean proportions had earned him the nickname of "Grande Jorasse", had found himself irresistibly overcome by sleep. And through their accounts ran the vague terror, which was kept alive by the relics of the ancient superstitions about the "Accursed Mountain". Jacques Balmat listened, and was confirmed in the decision he had already taken.

Working entirely on his own, he now gradually prepared himself to overcome every danger and obstacle the mountain might put in his way. He trained himself to detect the slight depression that betokens a crevasse, to appraise a wall which, seen from the front, appears impossible, to detect slopes prone to avalanche. His foot discovered the correct angle for walking on a slope in safety. His determination increased. The villagers made fun of him—"How do you think you're going to succeed by yourself," they said, "when all the others together have failed?"

And then came the great day.

Up till then the attempts had been made by two routes. One was by the Montagne de la Côte and the Vallée de la Neige[1] to the Grand Plateau; the other went directly up to the Aiguille du Goûter, then called the Aiguille Blanche, and it was in this latter direction that the final attempts were made. In Chamonix the merits of the two routes were hotly debated. There was general agreement that the Dôme du Goûter ought to be traversed, but one party thought it would be best attained by way of the Grand Plateau.

On 30 June 1786, a competition was organised between the two factions. Pierre Balmat and Jean-Marie Couttet spent the night at Pierre Ronde[2]; while Jean-Michel Cachat, called the Giant, François Paccard and Joseph Carrier slept on the Montagne de la Côte, to see which party would arrive first on the Dôme.

Just as the party of three was leaving the last chalets of Chamonix, they met Jacques Balmat coming down alone. He had been two days and two nights on the mountain during one of his fruitless attempts, and now he was returning after something of a struggle, judging by his clothes and appearance. These solitary expeditions of Balmat's to the glaciers of Mont Blanc, where every step was into the unknown, and every snow-bridge a potential death-trap, are among the most stirring pages in the history of mountaineering. And now Balmat was returning, but the meeting with the three guides going up disturbed him. Looking at Mont Blanc from the Brévent, he

---

[1] This was the name that de Saussure gave, in his *Voyages dans les Alpes*, to the route between the Grands Mulets and the Dôme du Goûter, as far as the Grand Plateau.

[2] On the Saint Gervais side, above the Bionnassay glacier.

had been sure that he had discovered something new, a possible solution of this problem, and he did not want the prize to be snatched from him at the last moment.

Back home, he ate, changed his clothes, and lay down for a few hours on his rough bed. But he could not rest, for mind, nerves and muscles were concentrated upon one purpose. Midnight saw him up again and on the way. At dawn he caught up with the three guides on the Montagne de la Côte, just as they were making ready to leave their bivouac, and he followed in their steps.

They seemed to be having the best of it, for they reached the Dôme well in advance of the Pierre Ronde contingent. Once the two parties had joined forces, they decided to return home. Balmat, who announced his intention of going on, was regarded as a lunatic. How could he dream of going alone in a place which they considered dangerous even when roped together? So they set off rapidly downhill, leaving Balmat to his fate.

Once again, he was thrown back on his own resources. At first he followed the slender crest, which became narrower and narrower, and when he no longer dared continue upright, he sat astride the ridge. In the end he had to admit defeat, and retrace his steps. But he did not give up, for this ridge was clearly not the only possible way. There was the route he had spotted from the Brévent. When he got back to the Dôme it was four in the afternoon; late in the day, certainly, but he did not care.

Down on the Grand Plateau, he returned to the Rochers Rouges, to the point by the bergschrund where, three days before, he had had to turn back at the foot of the great slope, which continued up for some 1,600 feet. He had not then dared to venture on the rickety snow-bridges because of the softness of the snow, but today, although it was late in the afternoon, the snow was hard; so without hesitation, he crossed the bergschrund and tackled the steep slope. He had been out for three consecutive days, had slept two nights in the open and spent the third walking. Only those who have been through similar experiences can understand what this means, and fully appreciate Balmat's formidable resolution. Up he climbed, step by step, breaking the snow with the point of his iron-shod pole. Then, quite suddenly, over the top of the slope, he saw the valley of Courmayeur. He had reached the shoulder of Mont Blanc and the day was won. Nothing now separated him from the summit, only a thousand feet above, except the gentle slopes of the final snow dome. Then, as if the mountain were calling up a last and deadly defence, down came the mist. Balmat no longer knew which way to go; night had fallen; back he went. In the darkness he was unable to cross the bergschrund, and so had to make a fourth bivouac. Snow began to fall; Balmat had neither tent nor sleeping-bag and his equipment, one may be sure, was very primitive. Beneath him lay the bottomless abyss of the great crevasse: over his head the gale whipped the summits and tore over the ridges, drawing the snow up in spirals and robbing him of breath. During the lulls in the storm, he could hear séracs crashing down, and all the noises of the glacier echoed and magnified by the surrounding mountains. After climbing all these thousands of feet, his limbs ached, and he longed for sleep. How many climbers since then have let themselves be caught in this trap! At the approach of the enchantress the blood seems to congeal, and eyes close in the sleep from which there is no waking. But Balmat was not yet beaten. He fought back with all his remaining strength, he beat his feet and waved his arms—there was no room to do any more. Dawn found him half frozen and almost blind from being so long on the glacier. He got down somehow, reached his barn, shut himself in and slept for twenty-four hours on end.

The right route had been found; but the summit had still to be attained. Balmat would have liked to return alone, but he was afraid he would not be believed by the others, so he looked about for a companion. He did not want another guide, and thought that Paccard might do—a strong young man, a doctor from Chamonix, who had given proof both of his ability and his ambition. They got together and, not even waiting for settled weather, set out secretly, without a word to anyone. At the point which Balmat had reached on his successful reconnaissance, Paccard was suddenly overcome with fatigue, and

Balmat tried to encourage him. But seeing it was no use, he went on alone. Step by step he forced the last defences of the peak—those last thousand feet, not very steep, yet perhaps the most tiring of all. The curve of the summit dome which blocked the view began to flatten out. A few more yards to go; then, suddenly, the slope dropped away on the other side, and there was no longer anything above him. The horizon opened out abruptly and the mountain ranges faded one by one into the distant haze. At that moment Balmat must have felt that the whole world lay at his feet. But he stayed there only a minute or two before running down again to rouse the drowsy and listless Paccard, whom he somehow managed to push and drag to the summit.[1]

Meanwhile at Chamonix someone had spotted the two black specks on the great white snow-cap, and a joyful peal of bells carried news of the victory from chalet to chalet. It was one of those victories which, small in themselves, mark an important stage in man's eternal striving to find, in the nobility of the struggle, the affirmation of his own heroic nature.

The vision of Balmat, aloft on the summit, faded in the darkness. The last strains of the distant orchestra were carried away on the cold breeze blowing off the glaciers. We returned to our modest hotel in the certain knowledge that we too would have the courage to battle our way along those storm-swept ridges.

Next day we went up to the Montenvers where we met Adolphe Rey, the famous Courmayeur guide, and Cairati Crivelli. We told Adolphe our plans, and he gave us a lot of useful advice about conditions on the mountains, which were still very bad. For our first expeditions in this new district we had, naturally, chosen three classic peaks: the Grépon, the Drus, and the Aiguille Verte. It would be two or three days

---

[1] Such, at least, is the original and legendary version of the first ascent as related by Balmat, and propagated by Alexandre Dumas. Recent research has since exposed the injustice of this fable and restored Dr Paccard once and for all to his rightful place. During the ascent Paccard played a part at least equal to that of Balmat; he took his share of breaking the trail, and arrived at the summit at the same time as Balmat. [*Translators' Note.*]

before the snow melted off the rocks of the first two peaks, so we
decided on the Verte, reckoning that the new snow would be
less of a hindrance on a route that was in any case on snow
and ice.

Next day we went with Rey's party to the Petit Charmoz,
a short training climb at the foot of the Aiguilles, then in the
afternoon we went up to the Couvercle hut which lies at the
foot of the south face of the Verte, and directly opposite the
north face of the Grandes Jorasses, at that time still unclimbed.

The Aiguille Verte, one of the classic peaks of the Mont
Blanc massif, forms the centre of a subsidiary group of summits
which rise from the lower end of the Mer de Glace, beginning
with the huge pillar of the Drus and, describing a wide arc
with the Droites and the Courtes, joining the main chain at
the Aiguille de Triolet. The normal route, by which the Verte
was first climbed, lies up the Whymper couloir. You leave
the hut at midnight by lantern light, and reach the summit at
dawn, in order to be down before the sun has had time to soften
the deadly slopes of the couloir and, if you've been quick, you
can be back at the hut in time for breakfast. At least so said
the Kurz and Vallot guide-books, and this was what we intended to do.

The famous guide, Armand Charlet, also left the hut at midnight with a client, but at the bergschrund he decided to turn
back. We asked him if he did so because the weather was
getting worse again, but he answered curtly that his client was
not in form, and vanished into the darkness, dragging his
Monsieur after him, and leaving us alone. We were still following some old tracks made by a party of Polish students, but
they had given up before reaching the great couloir because
of the quantity of soft snow, and where their tracks ended we
had to begin the strenuous work of breaking a trail.

As darkness gave way to an opaque light filtering through
thick mist, we moved slowly up. It was almost hot and,
although our feet were frozen because of the tightness of the
crampon straps, we sweated heavily. In the dark we had not
been able to get a clear picture of what lay higher up, but
now we began to gauge the depth of the loose snow from the

recent tracks of avalanches which had fallen during the last few days. To remain any longer in the couloir would have been extremely risky: to give the mountain up was something which, in my youthful enthusiasm, I did not for a moment consider. Moreover it is just these uncalled-for hours of struggle we look for in the mountains, and like best to remember.

The strength of a good fighter is increased by danger; it liberates him from the cares of the world, it frees him from the weight of his body. The demon that inspired Lammer now possessed us, and we followed where it led.

So, leaving the couloir and taking to the rocks on its true left, we continued to climb. In normal conditions these rocks are perfectly easy, but on this occasion they were interspersed with patches of steep snow which gave us a lot of trouble. We made the mistake of keeping on our crampons and found ourselves performing a series of desperate antics in a style that was anything but elegant!

Hours passed and our goal was still far off. There was no longer any question of enjoying the sunrise on the summit, nor of breakfasting down at the hut. When we reached the little col between the Grande Rocheuse and the Verte, it was 11 o'clock and the dead calm of the south face gave place to a wild north-westerly gale which met us on the ridge. The snow was blown up in spirals along the whole length of the north face, then spread out in long streamers on the far side. It was our first experience of those notorious Mont Blanc storms which so far we had only read about. We clung to the ridge with all our strength, groping our way along, and trying to keep clear of the huge cornice, which seemed to totter in the wind. Then we reached the summit, or what at least we supposed to be the summit, when we found that the ridge was beginning to descend. Without stopping we turned right about and followed our tracks back to a point under the little col where, sheltered from the wind, we stood on the steep slope and swallowed a little food before starting down.

According to all the authorities, there was no choice now but to look for a bivouac site on the rocks of the Grande Rocheuse, and to go down the following morning when the snow was

firmer. But a demon had got into me; and I still consider it
something of an achievement that we managed to descend
without mishap while the avalanches continuously thundered
past all round us. It was nine in the evening when we got back
to the Couvercle, dragging behind us a rope which the frost
had transformed into a tangled snake. We had to cut the knots
in order to unrope! But, somehow or other, we had brought
off our first ascent. Needless to say, on our return to Chamonix
we found the sun shining in a cloudless sky.

This was one of the many things I learnt about Mont Blanc
that season: down in the valley you loll about in glorious
weather; you start off on the long walk up to a hut beneath a
sun which doubles the weight of your sack, then, next day, you
wake to falling snow. You reckon it might be better to go
down while you wait for the snow to melt; then, after the two
or three days this takes, the game begins all over again. So
two days later we were back at the Montenvers *en route* for the
Grépon.

At 2 a.m. the stars looked down on the familiar sight of a
lantern swinging along the path to the Plan de l'Aiguille. As
usual we walked half asleep, thinking the thoughts one habitu-
ally thinks on such occasions. The Grépon, together with the
Drus, is among the most famous of all the rock peaks of Chamonix, and everyone who takes an interest in mountaineering
is sure to know its history, either from the writings of Mummery
who, with his usual humour, describes the three phases of a
mountain's evolution—an inaccessible peak, the hardest climb
in the Alps, an easy day for a lady—or from the over-dramatic
account of Guido Rey. Anyway, it remains a pleasant and
amusing climb on excellent rock, in surroundings of incomparable beauty. On this occasion, moreover, it was made
harder than usual and all the more interesting by the snow
which lined the cracks, and by patches of verglas. Consequently we were rather slower than the guide-book times,
but apart from this the ascent went without a hitch and we
were able to enjoy to the full all those famous pitches—the full
length of the Mummery Crack, the Râteau de Chèvres, the
Bôite aux Lettres, the Vire à Bicyclettes, the airy rappel from

the Grand Diable, and the strenuous final crack. All these pitches are so well in keeping with the special character of the climb that you would think they had been designed on purpose by an architect of genius for the exclusive use of climbers.

We had barely left the summit when the mist, which had already begun to drift round us, grew thicker and, just as we were about to set foot upon the Nantillons glacier, rain began to fall. At first it was a fine, close, almost autumnal drizzle, then it came down in a non-stop torrent. Soon we were so completely soaked that there no longer seemed to be any point in hurrying. When evening came we were still messing about on the Plan de l'Aiguille path, very fed up and convinced that this was the fate reserved for all our enterprises that year.

Lupotto began to tell me of the wonderful rocks of Portofino where, to judge from the way he talked, there would be a cutter awaiting us, gently rocked by the waves, and even a lovely girl sighing in the moonlight. His longing was increased when, at the Montenvers, two mountaineering pundits assured us that with the weather as changeable as this, the wisest thing would be to stay quietly down in the valley and wait for better days. But I was young and heedless, and turned a deaf ear to the voice of experience; and I managed to persuade my companion to follow me on one final adventure.

After two rest days in Chamonix we were off again; doubled under our enormous sacks we toiled up the abominable scree-slopes to the Charpoua hut, in the wild cirque formed by the great ice slopes of the south-west face of the Aiguille Verte and the red precipices of the Drus and the Pointe Petigax. But next morning the great Panjandrum of the Alps, no doubt irritated by our lack of respect for the established rules, decided to give us a lesson once and for all. He allowed us to leave the hut at dawn; he even let us have a bite on the summit of the Petit Dru, in the shadow of the statue of the Virgin; then, just as we were about to tackle the famous Z pitch which leads to the Grand Dru, he gave the signal for the great offensive. A vast black cloud came out from behind the Aiguilles, swallowed up the Grépon and descended to the Mer de Glace. The wind howled on the high narrow ridges and in the echoing couloirs, and the storm—one of those unexpected storms that climbers know so well—broke loose in all its violence. For a moment, we were nonplussed by such a sudden attack; then, since we could think of nothing better to do, we decided on an immediate retreat. But to descend the Petit Dru in such conditions is neither quick nor easy. We were still not far from the summit when hail began to fall in fierce squalls. Since rocky spikes attract electric discharges, the Drus is notorious for its lightning, and at once I remembered what happened to the Milanese party, Bramani, Bozzoli and Fumagalli, in similar circumstances. I reminded Lupotto of it, having no wish to keep my worries to myself, and he retaliated with a whole catalogue of accidents. Tongues of flame kept darting out of the cloud at the rocks all round us. While I was waiting my turn at one of the rappels I was struck on the elbow; my arm shot out like a spring, and the gloves which I had been holding in my hand went flying into space. The rope was wet and frozen and would no longer run through the rappel loops; I kept on having to climb up again to free it. I remember arriving at a small gap through which the wind blew with such force that we had to cling to the rock for fear of being blown away. I remember, too, a little couloir which we had to descend beneath a cascade of snow that fell in torrents from the rocks above.

Meanwhile the hail had turned to snow, and this made the rocks still harder. But, as we had no bivouac equipment, we made up our minds not to stop until we reached the hut. It took us more than nine hours to get down to the foot of the rocks, and though it was no longer snowing, there was still wind and low cloud. We had to find our ice-axes in the dark, for the wind blew the lantern out as soon as it was lit, but we nevertheless launched out on to the glacier, trusting to our instinct to find the way.

Lupotto went first, and as the rope ran out, he disappeared into the night. Tentatively I followed, with the rope coiled round the shaft of my axe, ready to belay. We wound up and down between the séracs, our only guide the pallor of the snow,

North face of the Civetta

Aiguille Noire de Peuterey

Cima Grande di Lavaredo

contrasting with the dark patches of the crevasses. We pushed
on in silence, determined to continue all night rather than stop,
for, wet as we were and with the icy wind still blowing fiercely,
a halt might well have been fatal. Suddenly a light appeared
down in the valley at the foot of the Aiguilles: no doubt someone going up from the Montenvers to the Requin hut. That
would keep us company.

Midnight, one o'clock. At two, without quite knowing how,
we reached the moraine. We had taken five hours to cross the
little Charpoua glacier; which on the way up had taken only
fifty minutes! In another half-hour we were at the hut. This
time it really was the end. Lupotto was off to Portofino, quite
determined to spend the rest of the summer in a boat. For
myself, I would return to my Carnic Alps, certain that the
Dolomites would be kinder to me in the matter of weather.

After this hazardous campaign in the Mont Blanc massif I
did not linger for long in the green pastures of Carnia. I was
obsessed by the wish to climb sound vertical rock, beneath a
sun which would efface the memory of the icy storms of the
four-thousanders, unencumbered by sack, ice-axe or crampons,
and with the elegance and lightness possible when wearing
espadrilles. Bruno Boiti joined me, and we set off again for the
Tre Cime di Lavaredo: as on our first visit, these peaks interested us, because on them we could make technical comparisons
between one route and another. This time the programme in-
cluded the Fehrmann, Preuss and Dülfer routes. I needed to
compare these routes in order to arrive at a clear and rational
estimate of my own powers; this would enable me to launch out
on more ambitious enterprises, and so to enjoy to the full the
boundless exhilaration which comes from living at full stretch.

From the Principe Umberto hut, we again climbed the Cima
Piccola by the ordinary route, then combined the first half of
the Witzenmann route with the Helversen route, then the
Witzenmann route with the Fehrmann. The weather was kind
and we were able to go on and do the Preuss route on the
Piccolissima. But while I was coming down the steep south
couloir in a series of rappels, I was hit on the foot by a stone—a

small incident, but it obliged us to give up the Dülfer route on the Cima Grande and return to Carnia.

My foot had barely recovered when we crossed the Col de Mauria once more to Domegge and went up to the Padua Hut among the Spalti di Toro; Bruno Boiti was in the party and a new friend of his, Giannino Agnoli. We set out at once for the climb which we then considered the hardest of the group: the Campanile Toro by the Piaz route. A well-known German party, who had succeeded brilliantly on the finest of all Dolomite climbs, the north face of the Civetta, had estimated the grading of this climb as "very severe".

In spite of mist and cold we got up successfully, and found it well within our capacities. During the following days the sun reappeared and we succeeded in making two new ascents: the north-west face of the Cima Toro, and the west-north-west face of the Cima Both; the latter is a very beautiful and elegant climb because of its extreme exposure and magnificent final chimney.

After this Boiti and Agnoli had to leave. I still had a few days in hand so I stayed on alone at the hut, enjoying a series of splendid September days, which live again in my memory, tinged with a gentle melancholy. I went out for long days by myself on the rocks, and felt at one with all the beauty around me. On the Campanile di Val Montanaia I climbed with the principal of a Salesian college at Belluno—the first time he had done anything so difficult. The last day there was a marvellous sunset, and it was marked by a phenomenon which I have rarely seen in the mountains. At the time I was in the high amphitheatre of the Cadini di Toro, at the upper limit of the shrubs and fir trees, and the sun was about to sink behind the Castello di Vedorcia. Only the Credola was still lit up. Then, in the crystal-clear air, a filmy mist rose up and met the last rays of the sun; against the light it looked like powdered gold, transforming the pinnacles into a fairyland. I felt I had been suddenly transported to the legendary kingdom of the Dolomites, peopled with goblins and fairies. Then, in a few minutes, the enchantment faded. The sun disappeared behind the Castello di Vedorcia; the golden dust vanished and the mist dissolved in the wind. For an instant the setting sun flamed red on the Credola; then there was nothing but the black of the fir-trees and the grey of the rocks. The tinkle of bells down in the distant valley marked the end of the day, and the end, too, of my mountain holidays for that year.

Two: 1932

Nordend of Monte Rosa—Winter mountaineering—Furggen ridge of the Matterhorn—Aiguille Verte—Aiguille du Moine—Dolomites: north-west wall of the Torre Coldai—North ridge of the Civetta—Videsott route on the Pan di Zucchero—West wall of the Torre Venezia—Attempt on the Solleder-Lettenbauer route on the Civetta—Pale di San Martino—Spigolo del Velo della Cima della Madona—Sass Maor, east wall

I SPENT the winter of 1932 in Turin, a period when we made bold resolutions and propounded great plans. In the course of my army training I had come to know the extreme southern tip of the great curve of the Alps—the Cottian and Maritime Alps —but my thoughts were still fixed on the Dolomites and the great Mont Blanc climbs. We talked mountains endlessly and our views and objectives became more clearly defined. There was no longer any question of solitary mountain wanderings for purely personal satisfaction; we had to give a more general value to our enterprises. I began to hope again that I might be able to realise the dreams I had had as a schoolboy, when I read of the great enthralling victories of man over Nature's fast-nesses, when Nansen, Amundsen and Scott had been my chosen heroes. My ambition was to follow the routes opened up by the Duke of the Abruzzi, and to push further in his tracks up the great virgin peaks of the Himalaya.

I knew very well that to prepare oneself for such a task was more than a question of acquiring the maximum technical competence; one would certainly also need to have had experience of high mountains under the most arduous conditions. These conditions would be found more particularly in winter, so when Emmanuele Andreis and Paolo Ceresa put forward the idea of an attempt on the Nordend—the second highest summit of Monte Rosa—I welcomed the suggestion enthusiastically. It was one of those climbs upon which the eyes and hopes of many parties had been fixed during the preceding years, but either because of bad conditions on the ridge, or bad weather, no one had so far been successful in making a winter ascent—or so it seemed, judging from information given in the Kurz guide and by other authorities on the mountain. It was only a few days after we had successfully climbed it that Andreis discovered the account of an ascent made by two Swiss guides with a client, in 1920, a winter very favourable to high mountaineering. During a long series of fine days the small quantity of snow that had fallen at the beginning of the winter had been swept away by the wind, and conditions on the mountain had been almost the same as in summer.

Towards the end of January Paolo Ceresa came round to tell me that Emmanuele Andreis wished to set out at once. As I too was free to leave town we made a rendezvous for the morning of February 3 on the first train leaving for Aosta. I succeeded in oversleeping and missed the train, so while my companions were well on their way, I found myself forced into a long pursuit which ended only at the Col de Théodule!

At Châtillon there was no bus service and it took a long time to collect three other people to share a taxi. I reached Valtournanche at 4 o'clock, and at the hotel I found a note from my two friends to say that they had left for the Théodule immediately after lunch, accompanied by Bich who had gone up with them to open the hut. "We'll expect you tomorrow at the col. Hurry up!" So, the day before the climb, I should have to go right up to the Bétemps hut in one stage! I didn't like this idea at all, and decided to go up to the Théodule by night: and I may remind my readers that the road to Breuil was not then constructed, and moreover there was not a single hotel open in the valley. Going up from Valtournanche to the col was, in fact, an expedition in itself, and no short one either.

When I left Valtournanche it was nearly 5 o'clock. There was no snow and I had to carry my skis as well as my already bulky pack in which were stowed rope, ice-axe, crampons and five days' food. Two hours of fast walking brought me to Breuil where I put on my skis and began to climb up to Giomein. From a hovel above the inn, which he looked after, there appeared the singular figure of Carrel, son of the great Jean-Antoine Carrel of Matterhorn fame, and sole inhabitant of this enormous plateau lost in its winter solitude. The old guide suspiciously asked where I was going, when the sun had already gone down and everything would soon be in darkness. I must admit that setting out on a long ski trip on a moonless night was something rather out of the ordinary, even for me. But I explained that I simply had to go up, and after shaking hands with him I went on my way, followed by his good wishes. I would certainly never regret this solitary midnight climb. Close of day in the mountains has always stirred me deeply, though I never quite know why. I went up unhurriedly, letting myself fall completely under the spell of the silence and splendour of the surroundings. The bulk of the Matterhorn was gradually blotted out by the night, while down below, at the entrance to the valley, the last gleams of an incredibly clear sunset died away.

When it became too dark for me to see the tracks made by my friends that afternoon, I lit the lantern and hooked it to my belt. By its flickering light I followed the faint indications, which barely showed at the turns on the wind-hardened snow. Now and again I missed the tracks and had to proceed by guesswork until, thankfully, I picked them up again. Half-way up the wind rose—this was annoying, for it was already intensely cold. To keep warm I increased my pace, but the first disagreeable effects soon began to make themselves felt. I had too tight a binding on my right ski and this restricted the movement of my foot; it began to hurt, and I suspected frost-bite. But the hut could not be far off and it was better to carry on.

It was just midnight when I reached it, and I was surprised to find Bich still up. After vigorously massaging my foot, I joined the others on the bunks: they were very pleased to see me, but rather surprised. "Tomorrow morning," they said, "we can leave early." But because we were lazy, and because it was so cold, we lay smothered under a pile of blankets, with our balaclavas on, until 8 o'clock. We managed to leave by ten, but we were in no hurry, for the way to the Bétemps would

be short and not very tiring. Instead of going round beneath
the Gandegg, we went straight down the steep slope leading to
the lower Théodule glacier. Maurice Bich had gone down to
the valley after shutting up the hut, so we were very much on
our own, completely isolated in the vast icy expanse of Monte
Rosa; this feeling of isolation is in itself one of the greatest
attractions of winter mountaineering. We made rapid progress
over the plateau of the great glacier which descends from the
Lysjoch, and soon there appeared on the right bank, at the
junction of the Monte Rosa and Grenz glaciers, a small black
cube lost among the boulders of the moraine—the Bétemps
hut, starting-point for our climb.

We reached the hut at two in the afternoon. After a quick
look round and a bite, the others decided to use the two remaining hours of daylight for a brief reconnaissance up the
moraine, leaving me to saw and chop wood, light the fire and
melt snow for water. When I had finished these chores, I sat
outside in the sun on a warm rock waiting for Paolo and Emmanuele to return. It was the first time I had been in this part
of the Alps. The Bétemps hut is set among the giants of the
Pennines, in the midst of the glaciers on their northern flanks.
It is surrounded by six summits of nearly 15,000 feet, as well as
by a number of other peaks of over 13,000 feet, which I recognised in turn from all the stories, old and new, I had read of
their conquest. I looked from one to the other and finally my
eyes came to rest on the rusty pyramid of the Matterhorn where,
a few days later, I was to be engaged in a grim struggle.

Meanwhile the sun was slowly sinking towards the Lyskamm,
and its slanting rays lit up the tumbled séracs. The high ridges
stood out in perfect purity of line against the azure sky. There
was no breath of wind; slowly the shadows spread over the
glacier. Until now my mind had been keyed up to grasp every
note in the mysterious harmony created by these wonderful
structures of rock and ice, but now, gently lulled by the surrounding silence, I began to relax and grow drowsy. The
crunch of nails roused me abruptly, and brought me to my
feet: the others had returned after climbing up the moraine
and reconnoitring the places which we should have to negotiate

by lantern light next morning. Now we had to think about food and sleep and we all went into the hut.

The next morning, February 5, we were ready to leave at 6.30. The cold was arctic, and there was not a cloud in the sky; everything promised well. Shouldering our skis, we made our way up the moraine; when we reached the glacier we put them on, roped up, and continued rapidly on our way. The snow was hard so that we could quite well have walked on foot, but the prospect of carrying our skis did not appeal to us and we managed to climb up by stamping hard on the snow until our edges gripped. Of course we should have been quicker walking, but then we should have had to abandon our skis, for they are very awkward to tow behind one; and suppose we were to find powder snow higher up? Such were the reflections exchanged at every zig-zag as the party made its way up this very moderate slope, where talking was an additional effort, not so much on account of the ascent, but because of the cold which gripped our jaws even through our thick balaclavas. There was as yet no snow on the glacier, which had been so well swept by the wind that areas of blue ice alternated with frozen névé. Finally, realising it was most unlikely that we should find any deep snow, we stuck our skis in a hole, and were all delighted at having taken this decision which saved us much weary trudging. We were fed up with having carried them so far and to no purpose—though we thought we might perhaps be able to make use of them on the lower part of the descent.

We put on crampons and climbed up more speedily. The route over the Monte Rosa glacier was the same as in summer, and was pretty obvious; it was only high up beneath the col that it appeared to be barred by some enormous séracs. We were still in shadow, but at the level of the Silbersattel a ray of sunlight shone through the gap and streamed out across the glacier, so we altered our course in that direction and as soon as we were in the sun we halted a moment, delighted to find there really was a slight difference in the temperature, and that we were able to warm ourselves up a bit. It was an hour to midday and we reckoned that we were within our scheduled time, in spite of the fact that the cold had made us drowsy, so that we had walked along half-asleep and quite incapable of increasing our pace. There was still another 1,300 feet to go before reaching the Silbersattel, and moreover we should have to contour round the crevassed area.

We continued the ascent, quickly leaving behind the providential ray of sunlight, but now, even in the shadow, the cold seemed less biting. On reaching the icefall we found, as we had expected, that the crevasses were all open, but some of the bridges were in excellent condition. It was only when we were very nearly through that an extra large crevasse forced us to make a detour in search of a place—the only one—where we could get across. Once over this difficulty we made the col with comparative ease and were then able to rest in the sun, which had at last reached this far. We now examined the ridge leading to the summit—it was some 200 yards long, and bare ice along its entire length, but fortunately not too narrow. It was here that we had to pay for the otherwise easy conditions on the mountain. There had been no snowfall heavy enough to cover it since the previous summer, so the ice was bare, and gleamed with a greenish tint—no doubt most artistic, but not at all to our liking in the circumstances.

After this pause we attacked. Mostly we moved together, but when the ridge got a bit steeper we prudently took some precautions. "A few steps won't do any harm!" I yelled to Emmanuele. "They'll come in handy on the way down." Anyway, whether because of the cold, or fatigue, or some other reason (God, what excuses!) I felt a bit shaky. The line of steps steadily advanced up the slope, and we proceeded in greater safety. At 1.30 we set foot on the summit, where a minute hummock of rock emerged, to lord it over the surrounding ice. The rock was warm—and very welcome too after so much cold. In the end it became too hot, so excessively hot that we felt an overwhelming desire for sleep. But we resisted the temptation and set about eating the few provisions in our rucksack —not without some regrets for the meagreness of the supply. Between mouthfuls we peered down at the formidable north face of glistening ice which was raked by avalanches. There was no doubt that it would need a great deal of courage to climb up that way, and we thought with respectful admiration of Imseng, the first to dare this wall and conquer it, regardless of falling stones and avalanches.

But the sun had now begun its downward course and we, too, had to think of the descent. We had been on the summit for an hour, rather too long considering the time at our disposal. Our first steps were even more uncertain than before. The sun and the unaccustomed height increased our torpor, and the flanks of the ridge now appeared to us to be most impressively steep and vertiginous, though this was really not the case at all —just an ill-timed joke on the part of the mountain. But gradually our confidence so far returned that when we reached the col we were running.

It was beginning to get late and we could not afford to hang about, so down we went at speed, halting now and again to recover breath. During the day the sun had softened the hard crust which now broke up under our weight into diamond-shaped slabs, but in spite of this we were not long getting back to our skis, which we put on in the hopes of a nice run down. This was not a good idea; after half an hour of incredible contortions we had lost barely three hundred feet in height and had to resign ourselves to taking them off yet again and carrying them down on our shoulders. Meanwhile the sun had disappeared behind the Lyskamm and darkness fell rapidly; our tiredness now began to tell, and we went more and more slowly. It was almost dark when we left the glacier and set foot on the moraine, and after half an hour's trudge through soft snow we had to light the lantern. By its flickering light we lost the tracks at once, and went on pretty well by guess-work in what we imagined to be the direction of the hut. We spent a good hour wandering about the boulders, shattering the silence with curses every time one of us fell into one of the holes lying in wait for us between the stones; and it was 7.30 when we reached our goal. We ate, and before going off to sleep drank a toast in sparkling—Vichy water!

On the 7th we started home, this time at last on our skis. We retraced our route of the 4th as far as the Théodule, and while my friends remained to do Castor or the Breithorn the following day, I went on down to Valtournanche. Here I was to meet Boccalate, Gallo and Pisone and my friend Lupotto, for an attempt on the Furggen ridge of the Matterhorn. In fact I found a note saying that their departure had been delayed. At the time I could not at all make out why, and it was not until I returned to Turin that I heard the explanation. As it was such a serious expedition, they had decided to follow the weather forecasts scientifically, and they diligently applied themselves to compiling daily information about the cyclones and anticyclones and their routes across central and southern Europe. The conclusion they drew from this study was that bad weather was rapidly approaching: hence their decision to wait. But after a few days, seeing that the information continued to be pessimistic while the weather persisted in remaining fine, we decided to carry on with our project. In the meantime, however, other engagements kept Pisone and Lupotto in Turin, and instead Guido Derege decided to join our party. The two ropes of two thus became a single rope of three, and on February 20 we took the train for Valtournanche. The same evening, beneath a full moon which made the valley almost as light as day, we reached Breuil where we spent the night at the new chalet-hotel, not yet completed, which Captain Bich had most kindly put at our disposal.

I feel that this is the moment to make a slight digression, in order to justify our intentions. In spite of the admirable successes of Italian pioneers from Sella to Piacenza, and the brilliant example of Marcel Kurz, there is still a very general prejudice in climbing circles against winter mountaineering. People are afraid of the difficulties, of the cold, and above all of the discomfort arising from the fact that the chalet-hotels are closed. But a climber who is strong and sure of himself should, on the contrary, prefer winter ascents, because these, more than any others, give him a chance of measuring his strength against mountains in severe conditions. They force him to battle without respite, completely on his own, day after day, and with no possibility of reprovisioning. Nowadays the judicious use of skis transforms the long tiring approaches to huts and to the foot of climbs into pleasant excursions, or fantastic descents, against a background of great mountains. Even optimists do not suggest attempting anything but classic summits by their normal routes; difficult rock routes are to be avoided. But among the many adverse aspects of the problem of winter ascents, there is one favourable factor: the virtual elimination of the objective danger of frequent stone-falls. Snow and cold, usually the climber's enemies, are in this case his allies, for they hold the stones fast in their icy grip and render these potential missiles harmless.

The Furggen ridge of the Matterhorn fits precisely into this category of ascents. At the time, this ridge had been climbed only twice: the first time in 1911 by Piacenza with Jean-Joseph Carrel; the second time by Benedetti with Louis Carrel and Maurice Bich.[1] An attempt to do this climb in winter might well be considered folly, and this was indeed borne out by events. But conditions in the mountains are not always the same, and a first experience may eventually turn out useful. It may be bitter to have to give up the realisation of an idea; but such a setback in no way detracts from the rightful satisfaction engendered by our passion, our enthusiasm, and our determination to win a victory over ourselves. And the moral value of defeat may even be superior to the satisfaction of a more easily won victory.

On Sunday morning we put on our skis and set out for the Hörnli hut. The weather looked promising: a light breeze blew from the north, and the mountains, rosy in the first rays of the sun, seemed to smile upon us. Our sacks were heavily laden with two ropes, crampons, ice-axes, and food for several days; and this, as well as the positively spring-like quality of the sun, slowed down our pace considerably. We took practically the whole day to reach the Hörnli over the Furggjoch.

On Monday morning at 6.30 we were ready to set out. To protect our boots from direct contact with the snow we drew woollen socks over them, and then strapped our crampons on over the lot. The weather was sulky, and we began to remember the unsatisfactory bulletins from Turin. Above the Ober-

---

[1] The first winter ascent was made in March 1948 by two Swiss climbers, Raymond Monney and Jean Fuchs. [*Translators' Note.*]

land peaks and the Monte Rosa massif light wisps of cloud seemed to forecast wind; threatening mists swirled round the top of the Matterhorn, broke away at regular intervals from the giant summit, straggled out and vanished into the sky, to be replaced by fresh mist billowing up from the far side. But the wind was from a good quarter, and our enthusiasm was proof against all depressions from the north. Moreover it was late—too late, as we unhappily came to realise—and we had to make a decision. So, muttering the usual formula to ward off bad luck, away we went.

We descended the moraine on to the glacier and attacked the east wall roughly at the base of a line dropped from the summit. This wall was still unclimbed, but as far as the ledge connecting the two shoulders, Hörnli and Furggen, the angle was not excessive. We gained height rapidly, moving unroped to save time on the steep slopes of frozen snow on which our crampons held admirably. Half-way up the face we began to cut across to the left, aiming for the foot of the second steep rise on the Furggen ridge. On this first stage, things seemed to go in our favour. Now and then a well-behaved stone, keeping a respectful distance, would bring us greetings from the summit; but happily the stones were few and far between—besides, the wall was so immense there was no reason why they should make straight for us.

At 10.30 we came to the first rocks of the Furggen ridge, six or seven hundred feet below the shoulder, and allowed ourselves a brief half-hour's halt for some food. The mists which most of the morning had veiled the sky had now disappeared— the result of a new moon, remarked Derege, our weather expert. Our confidence was justified: we were now sure of victory, for we thought we should reach the shoulder in little over half an hour. In fact it was only now that the mountain revealed the defence it was to raise against our determination to conquer. Above us the angle steepened, and the excellent snow which we had found hitherto was succeeded by large slabs of ice; so we roped up, and Gabriele took the lead on account of his greater climbing experience. We struggled on, but the rocks alongside were smooth and to climb them in crampons

required prodigious feats of virtuosity. Our progress was slow
and it soon became clear that we would not be able to reach
the shoulder in time to finish the ascent by the Furggen
overhangs.

It was 12.30; we decided to cut across to the right to the
Hörnli shoulder and spend the night at the Solvay hut. After
an extremely delicate traverse we reached the shoulder at
3 o'clock. The sun had sunk behind the mountain, the wind
had risen, and the cold was arctic. We went down the ridge
leading to the little Swiss hut, pausing now and again to warm
our hands which were in danger of frostbite from contact with
the rock. We arrived at 5 o'clock and made preparations for
the night, certain now that the fine weather would hold—it is
this certainty which enables one to undertake almost any big
ascent in winter.

On Tuesday morning we lay late under our blankets, thinking that we should not be able to attack the rock until it had
been warmed by the sun. This was our second mistake, and it
cost us the success of our plan. We left at 8 o'clock and climbed
rapidly up the ridge, which was clear of snow, reaching the
shoulder at 9.20. At first we followed our previous day's
tracks; then, after a couple of hundred yards, we abandoned
them and tried to make straight for the Furggen shoulder.
The difficulties were greater than the day before, for the sloping
ledge of loose stones which runs between the two shoulders was
covered with green ice and made one continuous and precipitous
surface with the steep wall beneath. Boccalatte had to cut steps
without a pause. There was absolutely no possibility of belaying, and this slowed us up, for a single false step by any one
of us would have resulted in our all diving headlong down the
wall up which we had climbed the previous day. At 11 o'clock
we were barely a third of the way across the traverse, so we
held a brief council. If we continued, it would mean a bivouac
on the Furggen ridge or, at best, on the summit of the Matterhorn; and at all costs we wanted to avoid a bivouac, for at this
time of year the consequences might have been disastrous.
Had we known then that we were fated to sleep out in the open
on the Hörnli ridge, it is probable that we would have pressed

on in spite of every difficulty; instead, we decided to retrace our steps, and climb to the summit by the Swiss ridge. At 11.50 we were back again on the Hörnli shoulder. After a ten-minute halt we left our sacks and began the last part of the ridge. Conditions were excellent, the rock was absolutely dry, the fixed ropes clear. On this easy ground our confidence returned and we climbed almost at the double. At 12.50 we were on the summit.

Looking at the immense panorama before us we forgot our misadventures, and the bitterness of not having succeeded on our chosen route. The meteorological expert pulled out a giant thermometer and announced the temperature: 10° Fahrenheit—almost mild, considering the height. We stretched ourselves out on the rocks to enjoy the pleasant warmth of the sun, but we could not afford to stay long and our halt was brief. At 1.30 we began the descent; making good speed, we reached the Solvay hut by 3.40. In twenty minutes we had collected the things left there in the morning, and after tidying the hut we set off down at 4.30. But little by little conditions on this side, which had appeared excellent, began to reveal themselves in their true light, for all the ledges that flank the ridge were iced and covered with fresh snow. We were forced to climb down carefully, always hoping that conditions would improve, but instead they became worse. At 6.30 we found ourselves on a sloping platform covered with frozen snow at a height of 12,500 feet, with the daylight beginning to fade. What was to be done? Continue the descent, relying on the full moon, or try to climb back again to the Solvay? After a moment's reflection we discarded both solutions. We might get held up by icy conditions on some pitch or other and be forced to bivouac in an impossible place; so we set about clearing the snow and ice that covered our platform, and after an hour it was ready. Night had fallen; far below the first lights of Zermatt appeared.

It would certainly have been more comfortable down there, but this made us all the prouder of being able to spend a winter's night on the Matterhorn. A small silk tent, a rock ledge, the icy wind blowing over the ridge, were enough to call forth the initiative and action which moulds and uplifts men.

But for the moment the temperature put a stop to further disquisitions on the marvellous potentialities of a human being. We gave a last glance at the countless stars which had gradually filled the sky and which seemed to smile encouragingly on us, and then we tried to get into the tent. It is by no means easy for three people to huddle into a tent made for two; so changing our tactics, we attempted to use the tent as a sleeping-bag, but it did not take us long to realise that this method would rapidly result in our being frozen to death. We tried the more normal method again and after considerable effort, and all working with a will, we succeeded in settling in, huddled close together with our knees doubled up to our chests. With the temperature at −10°, we began the interminable performance of getting through the night. Then came the first shiver of cold, the first feelings of apprehension. None of us had ever bivouacked in winter on a ridge at 13,000 feet, and this made it impossible for us to judge our powers of resistance accurately. But in face of this unknown element, upon which so much might depend, our determination to survive grew even stronger.

It was barely 10 o'clock: another nine hours before sunrise, so we sought for some diversion. We took all the provisions out of our sacks: a careful inventory revealed three dozen prunes and a few lumps of sugar. We divided the lot according to the number of hours still to go and decided to light the candle every hour, suck a few prunes, and make the business of sucking the stones last as long as possible. And at half-past every hour we would sing mountain songs to vary the programme.

To begin with these plans didn't work out too badly, but by 1 o'clock we had come to the end of both the prunes and our repertory of songs, and the six remaining hours passed somehow to the rhythmic accompaniment of chattering teeth. At the first faint glimmer of approaching dawn when the cold is most intense, we began to sing again. Another hour, and at last the red disc appeared above Monte Rosa, bringing with it warmth and life. We waited until the tent had warmed up a little in the life-giving rays, which it did very quickly on account of the confined space. Then we got out and began to dance a weird sort of ballet to restore the circulation to our numbed, cramped limbs. How delighted we were to have come through the ordeal! Without hurrying we packed our things, and it was 9 o'clock when we began the descent. We were very tired, and our throats were horribly dry, for our flasks had been empty for twenty-four hours. We reached the Hörnli in the afternoon, found our large sacks with the rest of our food, and decided to stay the night. So it was not until the following day, after having tidied up the hospitable little hut, that we climbed up to the Furggjoch on skis and returned to Breuil and Valtournanche.

After this most enjoyable winter expedition, our next task was to get ready for our summer campaign, which, needless to say, was to be divided between Mont Blanc and the Dolomites. I was to climb with Piero Zanetti in the Mont Blanc district, and Chamonix was to be our headquarters, but when the time arrived, Piero found he had to put off his departure for a few days. So I took the train by myself, hoping thus to force my friend not to delay too long. When I arrived at Chamonix I went to our usual hotel where I found Chabod and Boccalatte, who had come a week earlier. They had already climbed the east face of the Grépon, which they had found in bad condition, and were now preparing to leave for the traverse of the Aiguille Verte: up the Mummery couloir (the Y couloir) and down by the Whymper. When they heard that I was at a loose end for several days, they invited me to join them. So I was to be their "client".

I remembered the ascent of the Aiguille Verte well enough! The Whymper couloir with Emilio Lupotto had been like a bad dream, and I recalled little else except the midnight start, the ill-humour which suddenly came over us when we found that, owing to the warm wind, the snow was soft and sticky instead of hard and frozen and that our climb would inevitably take place in the worst possible conditions; the beginning of the climb with the snow increasingly deep and soft; the slowness of our ascent because of our having to take to the ice-glazed rocks to avoid the dangers of the couloir; the mist rising up in icy gusts; the beginning of the storm; the fierce squalls on the

final ridge that seemed to set the cornice shaking; the relief of
arriving on the summit and our immediate return without a
second's halt; the interminable descent and the infinite care
we took on the rotten snow which threatened to avalanche at
every step; the incessant fear that one of the avalanches hurtling
down the middle of the couloir would pluck us from the
extreme left-hand edge to which we were clinging and sweep
us away like straws; and finally our arrival on the glacier,
frozen through and through, blinded by the squalls of snow
and dazed by the ceaseless nervous tension.

So it was partly out of a wish to see this lovely mountain
in sunshine that I accepted the invitation. On July 2 we left
Chamonix to go up to the Charpoua hut which we reached
towards evening, after toiling up the interminable moraine,
covered with fresh snow. At 3 a.m. we set out by lantern light
to cross the glacier which, as usual, was very crevassed, but
well covered with snow as it was early in the season. This was,
however, only an illusory advantage for we sank in eight inches
or so and it slowed us up so much that we took over two hours
to reach the first of the two bergschrunds separating the upper
part of the glacier from the couloir.

We advanced slowly and in complete silence, and in the
darkness of the night my imagination conjured up fantastic
visions. I saw far back to the year 1881 when the first ascent
was made by Mummery with Alexander Burgener direct from
the Montenvers. I saw them toiling up the same glacier,
impatient to get to grips with the unknown which awaited
them in the twisting gully above. And I was both happy and
proud to be repeating one of Mummery's classic ascents, one
of those expeditions he undertook without fuss or glorification,
but with a heroic spirit equal, and often superior, to that of our
latest aces, accustomed as they are now to the all too frequent
use of artificial technique.

Eventually we came to the first bergschrund; it was almost
entirely blocked up and we had no difficulty in crossing it, and
the second was in exactly the same condition. Above it, the
angle of the slope in the lower part of the couloir gradually
increased over a distance of some six or seven hundred feet,

and we found this the steepest part of the whole climb. Actually this section did not resemble a couloir at all—it was more like a wall of ice with rock outcrops, and ended in a rock barrier above which started the couloir proper. We climbed up fairly rapidly, all moving together on the frozen snow, and avoiding the few rare patches of bare ice. When we came to the rocks we halted, reckoning the easiest passage would be in the middle, and we took off our crampons to climb a slab and a little couloir, the only difficulty being the verglas. We then continued up the rocks on the right before again taking to the couloir higher up. Just before leaving these rocks we came to a good ledge where we made a halt—owing to all the snow, this was the only relatively comfortable stopping place we found during the whole ascent. We would very much have liked to prolong our halt for a while—Chabod became unusually lyrical about the first rays of the sun playing on the surrounding peaks—but the intense cold soon drove us on.

We put on our crampons once more, and continued up in the direction of the large gap which we could see above, and also towards the sunlight which was gradually creeping down from the ridge as though to meet us. Although we were still moving together, we now had to go more slowly because I was beginning to get short of breath through lack of training. I was kept constantly aware, moreover, of the much vaunted superiority of the twelve-pointed Grivel crampons over my own modest ten-pointers. In fact, while my companions were able to go straight up using only the front part of their crampons, I had to resort to the more tiring method of flexing my ankles. A few steps cut here and there when we came to bare ice served to make our progress safer, and at last, 600 feet below the ridge, we came into the sun. In spite of the pleasure of feeling a little warmth after six long hours in an ice-box, we greeted it without enthusiasm, for the snow softened up in the sun and our pace consequently slackened. Before leaving the couloir we made over towards the right to avoid a large cornice; then, following the almost horizontal ridge, we gained the summit. It was so cold that we had to keep our gloves on while we ate, but that did not prevent us from prolonging our halt, for we had now given up all hope of making the descent on hard snow.

The Moine ridge has no objective dangers, but until the snow has cleared off this route the Verte remains something of a trap. Those who wish to do the climb safely by the normal route must ascend by night, arrive on the summit with the dawn and be back on the glacier by 10 o'clock. After this time, and above all if, as was the case on this occasion, there is a lot of snow, the descent is a very chancy affair. This was shown to be the case four days later when, in the upper part of the couloir, exactly where we had passed, the guide Devouassoux and his French client were swept away by an avalanche and killed. We began the descent at midday, and on the airy ridge leading to the Col de la Grande Rocheuse we quickly realised that crampons were useless; the soft sticky snow balled up between the points, making it dangerous to go on using them. So we took them off.

The Whymper couloir runs up to the col, and the first thousand feet are the most dangerous because there is no possibility of belaying. We went down together as quickly as possible, but it was hard work in the deep snow and, as soon as we could, we made straight over to the left where the rock rib coming from the Grande Rocheuse gave us a comforting security. We went on down, belaying each other in the usual way; from time to time a sudden crack like thunder made us halt and hold our breath as an avalanche, starting from one of the countless little side couloirs, thundered down the main gully, in one of the deep runnels furrowed in the snow by previous avalanches, and continued more silently, keeping to its channel, but frothing up whenever it encountered an obstacle. We watched its waves churning against the edges of the furrow until it vanished into the depths of the couloir, and this performance was repeated many times at regular intervals. We continued the descent, but before coming to the end of the couloir we had to cross one of these furrows. While the leader cut steps across the smooth, slippery bed, the other two kept watch. Then, moving all together, we crossed at the double. Once in the secondary couloir that runs down to the glacier on the left of the main one, we felt almost secure. Only the bergschrund remained to be negotiated. While I was peering over, looking for a bridge which ought to have been on the right, Chabod found it more fun to leap over it, gathering speed by glissading down the upper lip. This last manœuvre brought us down to the glacier, and at 7.30 we were at the Couvercle. We would have liked to drink a toast in a good bottle of wine, but in view of the tariff we had to be content with a half bottle between the three of us. To console ourselves we drank to the Grandes Jorasses, whose immense and formidable north wall faces the hut, insolent in its challenge. For how much longer, it remained to be seen.

Back in Chamonix we found Zanetti had just arrived and together we got ready to begin the programme we had drawn up earlier; but, as usual, bad weather took a hand and upset all our plans. The rain poured down in Chamonix, and on the mountains it snowed. Nevertheless the moment the sun re-appeared we set out for the Couvercle. In the afternoon, to pass the time, I went alone up the Aiguille du Moine—an enter-taining climb. From the summit I was admiring the sheer walls all around when my gaze was arrested by the faint line of a track descending from the Aiguille Verte. Lower down, however, not far beneath the col, the track vanished beneath the cone of an avalanche which had come from the Grande Rocheuse and had fanned out across the whole width of the couloir before petering out about halfway down the runnel. At the moment I did not attach much importance to this, thinking that the climbers who had made the track must have reached the hut long since. But as soon as I got down I learnt that no party had arrived, and that the guardian was in fact expecting a guide and his French client who were doing the north face from the Argentière hut. By evening fear of an accident, confirmed by what I had seen, had gradually become a certainty and the guides at the hut decided to leave in the morning to look for their colleague. We left with them at 4 o'clock. Alas, very soon the guides found the dead bodies of Devouassoux and his client below the bergschrund, and while

they prepared to bring them down, we went on towards the
Aiguilles Mummery and Ravanel, which we hoped to climb.
But before we had reached the foot of the rocks it began to
snow again, so we took our way back to Chamonix, in none
too good a humour.

For a few days we became ordinary summer visitors, and
rather bored ones at that, limiting our activity to the study of
the diverse types of people that surged in and out of Chamonix.
I have always been firmly convinced that man is without question the ugliest of all living creatures, but the specimens to be
observed at Chamonix defy the imagination. Eighty per cent
of the people one sees promenading the streets, and almost all
those who go up to the Montenvers to defile the glacier, seem
to have been sent there as exhibits of one particular type, all
dressed in the fashion most calculated to set off their ugliness.
Even the children follow the general rule.

We were utterly fed up, and for something to do we went up
to the Leschaux hut to visit Boccalatte and Chabod, and there
we found Ghiglione as well. Between showers the whole crowd
of us, except Chabod, went off to climb on the slabs above the
hut just to stretch our legs. We all roped up together, and I
started off in search of an interesting pitch. While I was coming down from an overhang which I had tried in vain to climb,
Boccalatte, who was at the other end of the rope, set off in another direction, going over to the right on to some steep slabs.
While he was in a layback position a hold suddenly broke and
he fell over backwards, hit the nape of his neck on the rock and
rolled over the edge. Zanetti quickly succeeded in hitching the
rope over a spike of rock, but was not able to save Boccalatte
from a nasty fall of about fifty feet. Zanetti held him all right,
and called to me to come over quickly. I hurried across to
join him, and then succeeded in making a delicate traverse
over the slabs to Boccalatte, who was unconscious, and managed
to drag him on to a ledge. At first we were rather horrified to
find that he had a large head wound which was bleeding pro-
fusely, but a quick examination convinced us that it was only
superficial. As soon as he came to, he began to question us; he
was amazed to find himself there, and could not make out why.

For a short time he had no recollection of what had happened, but he soon recovered and we were able to go down.

At the hut we bandaged him summarily, and he decided to return to Chamonix in case of complications. Seeing that there was little likelihood of being able to do any climbs, I had pretty well made up my mind to leave the Mont Blanc district and go to the Dolomites. So I accompanied Boccalatte down to the Montenvers, where we found friends, and among them the well-known climber Signorina Nini Pietrasanta,[1] who was also a qualified nurse and volunteered expert medical attention. Leaving my friend in her charge I went on down to Chamonix and thence by train to Turin and Frioul. After a few days in the Carnic Alps to get fresh equipment and to join up with Bruno Boiti, I moved on to the Dolomites.

This year the time had come for us to try ourselves out on some of the hardest climbs. In the post-war period from 1918 to 1925 there had been no developments in Dolomite climbing, and none of the ascents undertaken had surpassed the achievements of Paul Preuss, the technique of Hans Dülfer, whose invention of various rope manœuvres and piton belays was to open the way for modern exploits, or the great performances of Angelo Dibona with the Mayer brothers who, up to 1913, formed the strongest and best integrated party in the history of mountaineering.[2] Then, in 1925, Emil Solleder appeared in the Dolomites. Climbing technique had already made very definite progress in the Kaisergebirge, but, on account of the peculiar characteristics of those mountains, climbing there was rather like exercises on a training-ground. It remained to be seen who would have the pluck and initiative to apply this improved technique to the major unsolved problems of the great Dolomite faces. It fell to Solleder to play this role. In

---

[1] Signorina Pietrasanta married Boccalatte four years later, in 1936. Together they made the first ascent of the west face of the Aiguille Noire de Peuterey (1935) and of the east-north-east pillar of Mont Blanc du Tacul (1936). Boccalatte was killed by falling stones while attempting a new route on the Aiguille du Triolet in 1938. [*Translators' Note.*]

[2] Both the Young–Knubel and Ryan–Lochmatter parties made ascents before 1914 which were certainly equal, if not superior, to those of the Mayer–Dibona party. [*Translators' Note.*]

the Odle group he climbed the Furchetta from the north, suc-
ceeding where Dülfer had failed. Then he went to the Civetta.
The foremost climbers and guides had made numerous routes
on the northern escarpments—Antonio Dimai with British
climbers, Tomé with de Toni, and Haupt-Lömpel, who had
inaugurated a more direct route. But although all their efforts
were worthy of this stupendous wall, the real problem was
still very far from being solved. Even the extremely difficult
German route, which ascends direct to the Piccola Civetta,
lies entirely to the right of the hanging Cristallo glacier.
Solleder, however, attacked the wall at its maximum height,
where the line of ascent ran with beautiful directness from base
to summit, where the architecture was boldest and steepest.
The first time, with Lettenbauer and Göbel, he was driven
down after a struggle lasting thirty hours. But three days later,
leaving Göbel, still weak from an injury, at the hut, he reached
the summit alone, thus winning a great victory and making the
finest climb in the eastern Alps. Later, in the same year Solleder rounded off his list of ascents, which marked a definite
step forward in mountaineering achievement, with the east wall
of the Sass Maor.

So it was natural that we, too, should set our hearts on this
climb. It would establish my Alpine majority once and for all,
and thus give me the assurance that I was fit to tackle any
peak in the whole range of the Alps with full awareness of what
was involved.

Early in August 1932 I went up to the Coldai hut with Bruno
Boiti, and the following day we climbed Mont Coldai to get a
general view of the group and to do homage to the great wall.
I must admit that when I beheld the apparently endless series
of its tremendous precipices, I realised how lucky I was in
having been able to admire, within a few days, the two most
impressive structures reared by Nature on our continent for,
it seemed, the particular enjoyment of the climber.

Coming down from the Aiguille Verte, I had had the leisure
to admire the north face of the Grandes Jorasses, and now my
eyes wandered anxiously over this other supreme north face.
It is difficult to establish a true comparison. The then un-

climbed [1] north face of the Jorasses is undoubtedly more formidable and, above all, more forbidding. Sweeping up from a circle of chaotic glaciers, surrounded by great peaks, ceaselessly lashed by storms which streak it with snow and ice, scored by avalanches, the Grandes Jorasses represent the supreme challenge to the climber's nerve. The Civetta seemed altogether more harmonious—one might almost say, more amenable to conquest. Its natural setting contributed to this impression, with rhododendrons in flower on the rocky slopes running down towards Alleghe, whose clear emerald lake lies in the hollow of the valley. Both these great faces represent, each in its own way, the finest possible field that a mountaineer could hope for, to satisfy his ardent desire for struggle and adventure. The man who wins through to either summit and there at last relaxes, may well feel that his cup of happiness is full.

Bringing our contemplative reconnaissance to an end we made our way back to the hut, lingering here and there to pick edelweiss on the cliffs of Monte Coldai. We now had to make ready for the great assault. The following day we climbed the Torre Coldai by the north-west. From the summit we intended to examine the north ridge of the Civetta which we wished to climb before doing the wall, but mist prevented us from seeing anything, so we had to spend another day making a reconnaissance to the Castello di Alleghe.

The superb series of towers on the north ridge of the Civetta gave us a day full of sensational excitement. For nine hours we were continuously on the move; the climbing was sometimes easy and amusing, sometimes difficult and exacting all our attention, in ever-changing scenery, and always above the precipices of the north face, which plunged beneath our feet. We got back to the hut in the dark, tired but satisfied, and very conscious of the task that still lay ahead. But fate, or rather the chances and hazards we like to call fate, had decided otherwise and, by apparently contradictory means, it contrived a sequence of unforeseen events which resulted in my being thrown willy-nilly into a dramatic adventure.

[1] The north spur of the Pointe Michel Croz of the Grandes Jorasses was climbed in 1935 by the Germans Meier and Peters, and that of the Pointe Walker in 1939 by the Italians Cassin, Esposito and Tisoni.

The following morning Boiti was seized with a violent attack of colitis which put him completely out of action. A common enough mishap, one might think, but it turned out .to be all part of the game. We waited for two days, but things only grew worse; and meanwhile three German students arrived up at the hut. One day, for something to do, I persuaded them to come with me on the Pan di Zucchero by the Videsott route. They were not in good enough training and there was no question of my choosing one of them as a companion for the Civetta. We returned late; but meanwhile chance was still playing its hand, for early next morning, an hour before I got up, Vergilio Neri called in at the hut. He had come up from Zoldo, alone, and was on his way to the Vazzoler hut, to look for a climbing partner among a group from Trentino whom he had heard were up there. It would have been a wonderful opportunity to join up with him, but I did not learn of his visit until several days later.

Boiti made up his mind to go home, so we packed our sacks and went down to Calalzo. But I could not bring myself to give up the Civetta and, leaving my friend to make his own way to the Col Mauria, I continued to Pieve di Cadore in search of another acquaintance. I found him, but he did not wish to come with me. Instead he introduced me to a young German climber, Victor Schweiger, who had already done some notable climbs and who welcomed my suggestion enthusiastically. We decided to do a short climb together first in order to get acquainted on the rope; a young man called Antonelli joined us just for this trip, and we set out for the Coldai hut. This trial climb on the west wall of the Torre Venezia settled the matter—Schweiger was a very good climber, and impressed me most favourably. After Antonelli had gone we made our preparations for the Civetta.

Our first attempt came to a halt at the start of the climb. We found a party from Munich, who had come up direct from the Forcella Staulanza, at grips with the famous slanting crack. The leader had got up, but the second had come off, and was suspended beneath the overhang. It took him an hour to climb up the rope using Prusik loops, then they gave up the climb and both of them came down. By then it was too late to start, so we returned to the hut. Next morning at 3 a.m. we left the hut again. There had been a series of fine days, the weather looked set fair and with the wind in the north this seemed likely to continue. At 5.30 we were at the start of the climb; we changed into scarpetti and at 6 o'clock, in spite of my hands being frozen by the cold, I started up the very difficult first pitch; Schweiger joined me quickly. After the long crack came the great chimney. Here, too, Schweiger climbed the pitches quickly, but towards the top I noticed that for fear of losing time, and to make up for lack of technique, he was climbing on his arms, using up his strength and making tremendous efforts that would soon exhaust him. And in fact at the top of the chimney he felt his strength beginning to fail. We rested a little, then continued to the left by the Schmid variation. But as soon as the difficulties began again, he got cramp in his arms; his previous efforts had caused his muscles to contract, and the same trouble was starting up again. He could no longer use a hold safely, for his hands were half-closed and seemed to be semi-paralysed. We stopped again, this time on a broad ledge which bore signs of having been used for a bivouac. We had something to eat and I massaged Schweiger's arms.

Meanwhile, time was getting on. Schweiger wished to give up but I could not make up my mind to this. It was a wonderful day, the sky was crystal-clear and below the valley was smiling in the sunlight; I felt on top of my form, my greatest ambition as a mountaineer lay within my grasp, and the hardest part was already behind us. Everything might have been simple, direct, clear. But instead, gloom gradually descended upon us. After resting for an hour we made another attempt to continue, but at the first pitch Schweiger was all in. What was more, his decreasing strength had begun to affect his morale. I realised that it was no good and, without so much as a curse or a protest, though my heart was near to breaking, I let him down, and then joined him. We descended in silence. But the mountain knew that we were now defeated and that, though my strength was intact, I could do nothing against it;

as for Schweiger, he seemed to be falling more and more
beneath the mountain's spell. Panic on a face like this is a
terrifying business: I had already witnessed this particular
form of nerves, when no hold appears safe, arms and legs begin
to tremble, and everything seems to be spinning madly round.

To make matters worse, when we were above the chimney,
a shower of stones clattered down quite close as I was climbing
down to join Schweiger. I saw that the rope was no longer
being taken in, so I called to him to pay more attention, but
nothing happened. I descended quickly and found him at the
foot of the pitch with his head thrust under a rock and his
teeth chattering. It was clear that he had completely lost his
nerve. Below the chimney there are several rappels of eighty
to a hundred feet. With great difficulty I succeeded in getting
him down the first of these, then he refused to continue. I
begged, I threatened, but it was no good. The only thing I
could do was to lower him down the precipice like a sack, then
—always roped to him—to rope down myself. After I had
successfully repeated this manœuvre three times, we were
almost within reach of our immediate goal, which was the
easy, if tedious, scree-slope at the foot of the wall. All that
separated us from this was the initial slanting crack and the
rocks below it, some 250 feet high, by which one approaches
the climb. This time the manœuvre was complicated by the
fact that below the crack the wall overhung, and that Schweiger
would, for about sixty feet, be hanging free in space. Still, with
the rope running through two karabiners all would surely be
well.

Schweiger began the descent, and after a few yards he disappeared from view, swallowed up by the overhang. For some
moments I heard nothing except the noise made by the rope
running taut over the rock. Twenty, twenty-five, thirty, forty
. . . I counted the feet as they ran out; then the rope, which to
begin with lay in the crack, displaced a wedged boulder and got
underneath it. With the movement of the rope the boulder
settled back again and the rope jammed. Schweiger was now
hanging in mid-air right above the precipice. I tried in vain to
pull him up so as to free the rope. I tried again and again; the

jerks only resulted in increasing my companion's already desperate weakness. A choking cry from below begged me to "let the rope free". The situation was becoming more and more desperate every second. I unroped, and holding both ropes in my hand so as not to lose them, I went down to where the climbing rope was jammed and again made desperate efforts to jerk it free from the vice in which it was held. While I was trying to do this the rope suddenly slackened as though it had broken. I went over backwards and swung above the precipice, grasping the ropes above my head with my left hand only. I pulled up hand over hand for the few yards that separated me from the pitons, and then began to haul in the rope. It came easily and soon I had the empty loop between my fingers. "It's all over," I said out loud; then automatically I called out, and was answered by a groan. Feeling that he was being strangled by the rope, which had worked loose and slipped up round his neck, Schweiger, who was at the end of his tether, had completely lost his head. Without any cry or warning he had succeeded in getting one arm through the loop and had let himself drop into space. He fell twenty-five feet on to a ledge where his anorak providentially caught over a rock spike on sloping ground and checked him.

After I had sorted out the ropes, which had got horribly muddled during all these manœuvres, I quickly roped down to him and belayed him firmly with both ropes. A rapid examination revealed a compound fracture of one leg, and various body injuries. As soon as I had given some first-aid there was nothing for it but to go down to the Vazzoler hut and collect some other climbers to help me get him down. It was almost dark by the time I reached the hut, but I had the good fortune to find there several climbers from Trentino and Venice. I hastily swallowed some food and then accompanied by the best of them (including Virgilio Neri and Adriano Dal Lago), I set out again by lantern-light along the path to the Civetta. We arrived at the foot of the wall at 11 p.m. Up there Schweiger was shouting incoherently, in delirium. His condition was clearly so serious that we had, at all costs, to get up to him. We roped up in one party. All the exhaustion of those long hours

of effort followed by the break-neck race down the screes, disappeared in face of this renewed tension. There are times when
muscle is nothing but will-power, when one is conscious only
of an unwonted clarity of insight and force of decision.

Holding a torch between my teeth I climbed slowly up the
rocks—easy by daylight but very hard indeed at this time of
night—which led up to the base of the crack, then brought
up the rest of the party. We now had to get to the injured man,
who was about fifteen feet below us. It was a lengthy and
awkward business. Well held from above, I let myself down
until I could reach him, then I fastened him to another rope
and retrieved my two. The others pulled him up very gently
so as not to aggravate his injuries, while I, still held from
above, supported him. We got him up to a small gap where,
at 2 a.m. we laid him down on a ledge, and then there was
nothing to do but wait for daylight to get down the rocks at
the foot of the wall. Meanwhile Neri and Dal Lago set the
injured limb as best they could.

At the first signs of dawn we moved off. It was a long and
painful performance, and a terrible trial for the injured man.
At last we reached the scree where the other climbers were
awaiting us; they had bivouacked there and now took our
place for the tiring descent of the scree-slopes. Once down on
the path Schweiger was put on a mule which the guardian of
the hut had fortunately sent up. In fact he went on mule-back
all the way down to Cencenighe and thence by car to the
hospital at Belluno.

But I remained at the hut, and the mule had scarcely disappeared round the bend of the path when I flopped down on
a bunk and slept eighteen hours straight off. Next afternoon
I went off to the Coldai hut where I had to collect our sacks,
and once again I passed beneath the Civetta! The weather
was still magnificent, and the wall looked down in the brilliant
afternoon light, stately, immutable, and completely indifferent
to my presence, while I, a passionate and insignificant creature,
toiled all unnoticed up the screes which had accumulated stone
by stone, through the erosion of countless eras, under the
gigantic four-thousand foot wall. I was still desperately tired

and had to make frequent halts, during which I looked up at the final dark cracks high above—beyond the point we had reached. I felt that the mountain was looking at me as though it too was capable of emotion, was possessed with the same sense of a predestined duel between us of which I myself was conscious. I would return. But I knew it was all absurd, and that the whole idea of an opponent to be overcome was sheer imagination—a flight of fancy, prompted by some deep inner necessity. I knew that the accident itself had been due to chance, in just the same way that chance itself is the outcome of a certain chain of events. This is as it should be, and it is certainly better this way. For this reason, I would return to fight again.

From the Coldai hut I went down to Pieve di Cadore to leave Schweiger's sack and report that he had been taken to Belluno. Then I went along to the square, where the summer visitors take their pre-luncheon stroll. In the main café a few couples were dancing to the syncopated rhythm of a band. Feeling isolated, and out of place, I looked on as though at another world. My steps led me back to the road to Calalzo, but after a bit I realised that I was hungry so I sat down by the wayside and rummaged in my sack for the remains of my provisions, then went on till I came to the Hotel Marmarole. It was dark and, as there would be no more buses up to the Mauria Pass before morning, I decided to go into the hotel to ask for a room; but the manager, who was in evening dress, looked horrified. He was clearly offended by my even asking and sharply informed me that everything was booked right up. I of course had quite forgotten that my appearance must have been rather unprepossessing, and that with several days' growth of stubble, my coat all blood-stained, and various rents in my trousers, I must have looked more like a tramp than a gentleman. I bowed politely, and went off down the road to Piave and then up to Lorenzago. I realised that I was still living apart in my own dream world and that I could not yet return to the common light of everyday. I stopped at an empty barn; from a group of chalets in the distance came the sound of women's voices singing in harmony, making the evening gay. Lulled by their music, I fell asleep beneath the stars.

It looked as if my season's climbing would end with my adventure on the Civetta. But early in September, after I had returned to Turin, I found Boccalatte waiting for Signorina Pietrasanta, with whom he was going to the Dolomites. For a long time he had been keen to climb in that district, which he did not know at all, and I took advantage of this to draw up a programme that put the still vivid recollection of my defeat on the Civetta out of mind. The group we chose was the Pale di San Martino, but when we arrived at San Martino di Castrozza we found practically all the hotels were closed. Since we wished to climb the Spigolo del Velo on the Cima della Madonna, before going to the Pradidali hut, we bivouacked on the alp above Ronz. This climb, which we did with Signorina Pietrasanta, served to give our party training and rhythm. After a second night out beneath the fir-trees, which scented the air like musk, we went on to the Pradidali hut from which we could admire the scowling profile of the east wall of the Sass Maor on which Solleder had made one of his three famous climbs; this was the object of our visit.

We knew little about the climb except what we had read in the account of the second ascent by Brehm and Heckmair, which had appeared in a sporting journal with an introduction by Domenico Rudatis. In this account the two Bavarians spoke of pitches which demanded complicated rope tactics, of bulging holdless slabs, of subtleties in the art of climbing which could only be achieved by the most advanced technique. In view of the reputation of these two famous aces of the Munich school, this was enough to make us think very seriously. Gabriele, moreover, who had not yet been initiated into the secrets of modern limestone and dolomite climbing, had no very clear notion of the fundamentals and kept worrying me with requests for explanations about "long pitches of extreme and sustained difficulty", or "continually overhanging walls", and other phrases in current fashion which he had found in accounts of Dolomite climbs; by the time the reader has reached the end of one of these stories he can no longer understand how there can possibly be any mountain left, considering the angle at which the walls are tipped! I replied evasively, anxious not to commit myself, but in the end I had to admit that really these accounts did seem to me rather exaggerated.

We spent an enjoyable day lazing and talking pleasantly of one thing and another, and left the hut on the morning of September 18. Although rather late in the season it was almost hot. Beneath us floated a magnificent sea of cloud from which emerged summits both near and far, shining clear as day in the light of the moon. We went quickly down with Signorina Pietrasanta, who gave us the pleasure of her company as far as the foot of the climb. Gradually we were engulfed in the mists which filled the valley. On a level with the foot of the wall the mule-path ran across steep slopes, then over the stone-shoot coming from the deep gorge to the right of the Sass Maor. We followed the path for a little way beyond the stone-shoot, then diverged and went a short distance up the scree among dwarf pines until we came to a ledge at the beginning of the rock terraces, which led us to the foot of the wall proper.

For over half an hour we wandered from ledge to ledge before we succeeded in finding the correct route about 300 feet above the start of the climb. We stopped to take off our boots and put on espadrilles, then continued slowly over easy rock and soon came to the beginning of the series of chimneys that cuts obliquely across the face and leads to the central corner groove. Here we stopped again, this time to make a good meal and thus lighten the sack, which, regardless of consequences, had been very well filled. Our feeling of isolation was increased by the mist which again swirled beneath us, completely blotting out the valley. But above it was sunny, and the mountain seemed to invite us up. We stopped for about half an hour, eating slowly, as if to prolong the last peaceful moments before going into action; then we began the climb.

We quickly climbed the chimneys, and then came the first real difficulties: a vertical crack of some fifteen to twenty feet, followed by a typical little yellow wall consisting of broken-up triangular slabs of rock. Above, the corner groove ran up vertically, with formidable overhangs. Seen from below the wall appeared unclimbable. With happy intuition Solleder had turned the difficulties on the right, leaving the groove and returning to it again higher up, which entailed two excessively hard traverses. These pitches constitute the main difficulties of the whole climb and they are, in my opinion, slightly harder than the first pitches of the direct route on the Civetta. Above the little wall a ledge ran round to the right and then ended abruptly at a big block. At the far end of this ledge, and leaning up against the block, was a small wall of stones—clear evidence of a bivouac—probably left by Carlesso and Caserta, who had that year made the third (and first Italian) ascent of the wall; they had been caught in two storms and had had to spend the night on the mountain. After the ledge the yellow, practically vertical, and apparently holdless wall dropped away precipitously. Before embarking on the pitch I made a detailed examination in an attempt to pick out the line of least resistance. From the ledge one had to traverse out to the right, at first horizontally, then obliquely upwards in order to reach a rock spike that stuck up from a yellow rib. Finally I took the plunge. One had to trust to minute hand and foot holds which appeared only as one moved up and out over the maximum possible exposure. Spaced far apart there were more pronounced rugosities which gave some resting-places. When I reached the spike I had run out nearly all the rope and I stopped to bring up my companion. A few yards beyond the rib I caught sight of another piton. I reached it by a traverse, put on a running belay, and then climbed up by a scoop in which there was a very narrow crack only just wide enough for the fingers. This second pitch of roughly eighty feet is perhaps the hardest on the climb, and certainly the one requiring the greatest combined effort. On the whole traverse there was never any question or need for rope manœuvres.

And so we came to a little step beneath an overhang. On the right there was a gap in the overhang with excellent handholds which made it possible to get up. Above, the angle of the

wall relented slightly for a rope's length, after which we had to
go back to the left and return to the corner groove which,
from below, appeared to be deep and furrowed by chimneys.
There followed some very broken rocks and, after a little alcove,
an almost horizontal crack in which we thrust our hands,
placing our feet on minute rugosities while the whole body
hung out above the precipice. After about forty feet the crack
came to an end. The upper part of the wall receded, while the
lower lip continued and formed a little ledge. I managed to
get on to it after surmounting an exhausting overhang. Thirty
feet beyond the overhang I stopped to belay. Knowing my
friend's ability I did not take the precaution of putting in a
piton, but contented myself with running the rope over the
edge of the ledge; and we very nearly paid dearly for this lack
of caution. Arrived below the overhang Gabriele tired himself out unclipping the karabiner, and when he came to climb
the pitch he could not get up. I could give him no help, for
I was not directly above him and the rope came up diagonally.
If he had fallen he would have swung right across beneath the
great overhang of the wall, with a drop of nearly a thousand
feet beneath him. I watched his efforts, powerless to help,
and feeling worried about my own position in the event of his
falling. With no hope of pulling him up I might have been
able to hold out for an hour, perhaps two, then I should have
been faced with the choice of two possibilities: to let myself
slip over the edge or to cut the rope. . . . I felt my strength
ebbing. Gabriele had left the karabiner on his rope and with
great presence of mind he succeeded in clipping it back into
the piton and at once let himself slide down. He was thus able
to descend a few feet, and after a rest he negotiated the pitch
successfully.

The ledge continued and we followed it though it was narrow, broken up and difficult, and the climbing often delicate
and exposed. Further on it broadened and brought us back
into the corner groove. Here the first pitch consisted of a large,
very steep, rough-textured slab broken by a sort of cupola which
we avoided. After a balance move across a final smooth, interesting slab, and a pitch on some whitish-coloured rocks we

came out on to a comfortable platform at the foot of a chimney. As far as we knew the main difficulties were over, so, as it was quite early and the rest of the climb did not cause us any anxiety, we downed tools.

A mountaineer always adapts himself to the peculiarities of his climb and to the weather conditions. He is light-hearted and happy when the unknown element of the climb consists only in subjective difficulties; but when the mountain begins to threaten him with its objective dangers, when the storm rages, then his mood becomes gloomy and fierce, as though some devil urged him to hit out and battle with the raging elements. Then climbing becomes a desperate struggle.

Today, apart from the passing shadow thrown by our moment of suspense, now happily over, our climb belonged to the former category, and we could now peacefully enjoy a well-earned rest with our pipes on an airy perch, sorting out the impressions made by the climb so far. An hour passed pleasantly, and then we had to be off again. The difficulties now seemed slight in comparison with what had gone before, and we moved up rapidly, though only one at a time. We climbed two successive chimneys and then a third one, very characteristic, which narrowed towards the top and from which we emerged through a hole. After this there was one last steep portion followed by easy rocks. We made over to the left up a small enclosed slanting gully, easily visible from the foot of the wall, and then came out on to the crest some fifty yards from the top. And so along the ridge to the summit.

It was four in the afternoon. We rested about an hour enjoying the mist effects and singing out of sheer happiness. After a brief discussion we decided to go straight down to the gap between the Sass Maor and the Cima della Madonna, in order to reach the chimney which we had already descended a few days before on our way back from the Spigolo del Velo; then, at the foot of the rocks we would stop for the night. Our vile bodies would certainly have preferred good beds at San Martino di Castrozza, but already during our short stay among the mountains of San Martino, we had slept out twice in the open just near the alp above Ronz, and we felt that a third time would make a good round number, so we duly renounced the beds.

Finding a convenient site at 6.30, we set about putting our plan into practice. Twilight had not yet fallen, and we sat down on two large stones to await its coming. After a great climb, it doubles one's pleasure to rest like this, still apart from the world. It was absolutely quiet, and as we looked into the far distance, the impressions we had gathered on our climb seemed to be prolonged and multiplied. The westering sun gilded the mists slowly rising to engulf the summit. The exhilaration of the struggle died down within us, and when darkness fell we were filled with a deep longing for other battles, other conquests, other mountains.

When the last gleams of light had faded behind the peaks opposite, the damp cold of the night air brought us down to earth and we pulled on our sleeping-bags. Tomorrow we would go down to the valley happier men for having widened our experience and enriched our memories with all these new impressions.

Three : 1933

CLIMBING in the Western Alps had come to a standstill during the last few years compared with the developments taking place in the Eastern Alps—a very understandable phenomenon when one considers such factors as the tremendous variety of conditions in which climbs are undertaken in the Western Alps, and the consequent extra weight of equipment. Nor can people embark on these climbs with quite such an easy mind, for the objective dangers are far greater.

It was not until 1931 that it fell to Brendel and Schaller to make the first ascent of the south ridge of the Aiguille Noire de Peuterey; this was a western climb of equal importance, both in conception and execution, to the ascent of the Civetta in the Dolomites, and it was a decisive step towards the greatest Alpine climbs. In the Eastern Alps, the application of the new techniques—whereby even moderate climbers were able to undertake first-class climbs—and the more stable weather conditions, had led to a spate of new routes of extreme difficulty. But local conditions in the Western Alps, which added to the material difficulties as well as having an effect on the climber's morale, delayed a similar development.

By the summer of 1933 the south ridge of the Aiguille Noire had not been repeated, and it was still the only pure rock climb of first-class standard in the Western Alps. So it was with the firm intention of repeating this route that I went off to Courmayeur early in July.

Towards the end of June I had been to the Dolomites with Piero Zanetti, Massimo Mila and Gianni Colonnetti to get

quickly into training. Among the climbs we did were the
Vajolet Towers and the Spigolo of the Punta Fiammes.

While we were waiting at Courmayeur for the arrival of Piero
Zanetti who, as usual, was several days late, I went off with
Boccalatte to do the Pointe Gamba. This is the first big gendarme on the ridge of the Aiguille Noire and is in itself a
summit; from it we were able to examine the first part of this
long ascent. Then when Zanetti arrived we made up a large
party and traversed the Rochers de la Brenva, an amusing
training trip.

A few days later we went up to the Torino hut with Boccalatte and Nini Pietrasanta to do the Aiguilles du Diable. We
left the hut on July 24 at 2 a.m. and made such good speed
on the frozen crunchy snow that we reached the bergschrund
at the foot of the Col du Diable too early and had to wait
half an hour for the first light of dawn. At 6.20 we were at the
gap between the Corne du Diable and the Pointe Chaubert,
and at 7 o'clock we attacked the rocks. It is a long and enter-
taining climb over the crests of these slender needles with some
daring rappels between; our only troubles were the bother of
changing from boots to scarpetti, the hard going at the gaps,
which were still thick with fresh snow, and the ice and verglas
on the Pointe Carmen. Round us lay a world of savage beauty.
Seen from here Mont Maudit, with its fantastic carapace of
snow and ice, looks like a Himalayan peak. Climbing slowly
up its south-east ridge—the frontier ridge—was a party from
Geneva, led by Marullaz, which had left the hut at the same
time as ourselves. They, too, were finding it hard work because
of the quantity of snow.

When we came to the Isolée we had to give up any idea of
climbing it, for there was verglas in the crack and the slab
above was completely covered in snow. We waited for Boccalatte and Signorina Pietrasanta, and after a long halt went on
together to the summit of Mont Blanc du Tacul, which we
reached at 6 p.m.

We were very late and we tried to make up for this on the
descent, but beneath the Col du Midi we broke through the
top crust of snow and this slowed us up again, so that by the

time we came to the great ice-fall it was dark. For a while
we wandered about by lantern-light among the crevasses, till
finally Boccalatte found some tracks and we toiled up the last
familiar slope beneath Les Flambeaux to reach the hut at
11 p.m.

On July 30 Zanetti and I decided to go up to the Noire hut,
determined to attempt the great south ridge which no one
had yet repeated. As you approach Courmayeur from Pré-
Saint-Didier, the Aiguille Noire appears to be a mere fore-
ground detail in the immense picture of Mont Blanc. Yet even
then, when the light is favourable, you can make out the bold
sweep of the huge bastion of its south ridge. By the time you
reach Entrèves, and better still if you push on as far as Planpincieux, the detail has become a major part of the monu-
mental Peuterey ridge of Mont Blanc. It is in fact the first
upsurge of this immense ridge whose architectural design it out-
lines and emphasises. But when you get closer, and look at it
from under the western precipices or from the Fauteuil des
Allemands, Mont Blanc disappears from sight and you are then
left speechless, almost overwhelmed, by the tremendous impact
of the succession of slabs, polished and blackened by water, and
by the yellow walls sweeping up three thousand feet and more
above your head.

These were the impressions with which, on July 30, Zanetti
and I arrived at the little Aiguille Noire hut—a small wooden
box backing up against the rock in a great cwm scooped out of
the flank of the mountain. The approach is most attractive:
leaving the Peuterey chalets you cross the moraines under a
huge bastion furrowed by waterfalls, climb up this steep wall
—there are several regular pitches—and cross the stream twice.
The angle of the wall gradually lessens and you emerge into a
hanging valley whose name, Fauteuil des Allemands, describes
it to perfection. Up there we found some sheep, which are
brought up in the spring and left to run wild all through the
summer, and the whole flock followed us to the hut. They were
there again next morning when we left the hut at 4 a.m., and
escorted us as far as the tongue of snow beneath the Pic
Gamba.

There, as the ascent is all on rock, like a Dolomite climb, we changed into espadrilles and left our boots at the foot. With the first light of dawn we started up the rock face of the Pic Gamba, traversed to the right along a ledge and then made straight for the Welzenbach, by-passing the little gap between it and the Gamba—a small variation which only wastes time and is not to be recommended. By easy rocks we climbed to the elegant ridge leading up to the two gendarmes below the Welzenbach, and just as we reached this ridge a thin white mist gradually spread over the sky. Zanetti at once began to counsel caution. He declared that it was an unmistakable sign of bad weather, and while we halted briefly he told me in great detail about the dramatic adventure of Ottoz, Grivel and the others who had been caught in a storm beneath the fourth tower, the Pointe Brendel. I maintained that in this case it was merely the wind, but as we were uncertain we decided to beat a retreat and wait until the following day. However, before going down we made a wager: the stake was a bottle of sparkling wine, to be drunk in Courmayeur. If the weather remained fine Zanetti would buy it, and he declared he would be happy to lose; on the other hand, if the weather turned bad not only would I miss my climb, but I should have to pay for the wine as well.

We went back to the hut in the afternoon and lay down on the bunks, and when we got up for supper the sky had cleared. At 5 o'clock next morning we returned to the attack. I was doubly happy, to have won my bet and to be back on the ridge.

Although not very difficult, the first part of the climb is rather long, and we did not reach the summit of the Welzenbach until 11 o'clock. The splendid climb up the great rock rib to the two gendarmes, well supplied with holds on sound rock and with some beautiful pitches, fully came up to our expectations.

We remained for nearly an hour on the Pointe Welzenbach, for the weather was brilliantly fine and it was a delight to relax and admire the view of this side of Mont Blanc between the Brouillard and Peuterey ridges. But our attention, and our conversation, were mainly concerned with the red cliffs of the ridge ahead of us. Seen full on like this the fourth and fifth towers looked as if they would offer continuously difficult climbing. Brendel and Schaller had certainly given a rather alarming description of the dièdre and its exit.

At midday we moved on again, roping down into the gap between the Welzenbach and the Brendel[1] and then attacking the demi-lune on the fourth tower. Pitch after pitch followed, each one finer than the last, and we had to put everything we knew into climbing the famous dièdre on the fifth tower, where the exit is made by a balance move. With the fifth tower in the bag, success was certain.

After one more really hard pitch below the Pointe Bich the difficulties eased off. But meanwhile the afternoon had flown by and the sun had already disappeared behind the Brouillard ridge. Some 250 feet below the summit we discovered a marvellous bivouac site sheltered from the north wind, and though there was still another hour of daylight, we decided firmly to stop where we were. We stretched out at full length between two big boulders; undoubtedly it was the most comfortable bivouac I have ever had on a big climb. We finished our provisions and then slipped into our sleeping-bags. It was quite mild, the moon was high in the sky, and while Pierre recited poetry I gave rein to my imagination and so forgot the discomfort of my stony bed. Mountaineers are often accused of shooting a line when, snug at home in winter, from the depths of a comfortable armchair, they sing the praises of bivouacs. Perhaps it is true. But isn't it also true that in life the experiences we value most are those which leave their mark most deeply on us? Long periods can go by without making any impression —days all alike, all empty, days one reckons a complete loss, when one feels one hasn't really been alive. But these other days remain indelibly fixed in our memory, and bring the tang of a more heroic life into the petty hypocrisies of the daily round.

The first rays of the sun brought us out of our sleeping-bags, and after a few warming-up exercises we continued the climb.

_____
[1] After this rappel the party is more or less committed to continuing the climb.

After the Pointe Bich we came to the final summit of the Aiguille Noire. There was no hurry and we lingered a little before beginning the descent. By evening we were down in Purtud where we had supper before returning to Courmayeur.

Our partnership had successfully passed its qualifying test with the ascent of the south ridge of the Noire, which was the climax of the careful preparation begun in the Dolomites at the end of June. Now we could turn with confidence towards the object of our secret ambitions. On August 8 we crossed the Col du Géant to Chamonix, where we stayed just as long as was necessary to stock up with a week's provisions. Then, laden like mules, we made our way up to the Leschaux hut, a small wooden building on the right bank of the great glacier of that name, directly opposite the wall of the Grandes Jorasses.

There are few mountains with a reputation to touch that of the north face of the Grandes Jorasses—a reputation which arose, of course, from the fact that many of the best mountaineers in the world had failed in their attempts upon it. It was defended not only by its exceptional situation, and by the actual difficulties; there was a psychological reason as well, through the awe it inspired.

In the golden age of mountaineering—that is to say the pre-war years from about 1907 to 1912, the years of Dibona, the Lochmatters and Knubel—one or other of these parties must undoubtedly have passed beneath the wall and looked up to the summit, not just in admiration, but to pick out a possible route.[1] But it was not until 1928 that any real attempt was recorded. That year two parties—the guides Armand Charlet of Chamonix and Elisée Croux of Courmayeur with Rand Herron, Piero Zanetti and Poldo Gasparotto—attacked the lower buttress of the Walker spur. They succeeded in getting up the first steep ice slope, then they went round, to the left of the smooth slabs, and into a chimney up which they climbed. But at the exit of the chimney they were stopped by a holdless vertical dièdre which would have demanded modern piton

[1] In fact Geoffrey Young with Joseph Knubel climbed some way up the central spur in 1907. [*Translators' Note*.]

technique. So, after only six or seven hundred feet, they were forced to come down, horribly impressed by the frequent stone-falls which rake the wall. Time went by; the wall—the "great problem"—kept cropping up in the conversations of climbers, and the best of them all nursed the secret ambition of coming to grips with *the* North Face. Then came the Germans who, with their Munich group, were at that time the leaders in the evolution of Alpine technique. Brehm and Rittler launched their attack up the great central couloir: they were found at the foot of the wall, possibly the victims of an avalanche, or of a slip on this desperately steep slope. Kröner and Heckmair crossed the great bergschrund and then at once retreated. Franz and Toni Schmid, Welzenbach, Steinauer, all spent a long time in the neighbourhood, without being able to start on the climb.

In 1932 Boccalatte and Chabod made a reconnaissance of the start of the Walker spur, while Carrel and Crétier, with Bich and Benedetti, succeeded in climbing up for about three hundred feet on the right of the spur. At the beginning of this year two of the competitors were killed while getting into training. Toni Schmid fell on the Wiesbachhorn, and Amilcare Crétier was killed with two youthful companions, not on the sort of climb that would have done justice to his enterprise, but as the result of a commonplace and inexplicable accident on the descent of the familiar Matterhorn. Everything conspired to throw a fatal aura over the wall, and it is easy to imagine how its terrible reputation affected the morale of climbers getting ready for a merciless struggle with the Jorasses.

Though we shared in this general depression of spirit, we were still absolutely determined to win through when we established our little base camp in readiness for the great assault. We were in no great hurry, for the weather was uncertain, and we settled down to a long and careful study of a possible route through the powerful field-glasses I had brought with me.

Two gigantic ribs run up the north face of the Grandes Jorasses, starting from the chaotic Leschaux glacier and terminating in the Pointe Walker and Pointe Croz. They are about five hundred yards apart and lie either side of the great central slope. To the east of the Walker spur the wall is bounded by the steeply-angled Hirondelles ridge; on the west it is prolonged in an imposing rampart as far as the Col des Grandes Jorasses, nearly half a mile away. The wall, which is over 3,000 feet high at its central point, reaches its maximum height at the two spurs, the 4,000 foot Walker being the higher.

Piero inclined to the Walker spur as a line of ascent; this route, as well as being the finest and most considerable, led to the highest summit of the Jorasses, and would be a proper sequel to his previous attempt. But as a result of my observations, I was beginning to feel convinced that the central spur, leading up to the Pointe Croz, was the more accessible. Later events bore this out. My choice of route was based not so much on difference of difficulty, as on the fact that it faced more to the west, had more of the afternoon sun, and was consequently less encumbered with snow and ice.

Three days went by in observation, reconnaissance and preliminary sorties, while the weather behaved in a very odd manner that did little to reassure us. During the day large threatening clouds entirely covered the Aiguille de Leschaux, the Col des Hirondelles and part of our face; late in the afternoon these disappeared from the Jorasses basin, while storm-clouds massed over Mont Blanc. Had we been positive that the weather would go on like this, we might have made a start, but there was no means of telling, and with so serious an undertaking we were determined to avoid, as far as possible, any sudden surprise in that quarter. So every evening we made up our minds to start, but when we got up at 1 o'clock, the sight of the wall half-covered in cloud sent us back to our bunks. By midday all would be clear and we would blame ourselves bitterly for not having come to the point. Then, in the evening it would be the same old story over again. Our stay at the Leschaux hut was far from disagreeable. No one came to disturb our solitude, no one knew of our intended attempt. From time to time we saw parties coming up the glacier, but they always went off towards the Couvercle. Giving free rein to our imaginations, we would fancy ourselves completely isolated in an unknown world, knights in quest of hidden treasure, or on

the track of a fabulous monster, and such agreeable fantasies
seemed to enhance the reality. The evening light over Mont
Blanc fringed the clouds with gold, and we were touched by
the melancholy which accompanies sunset in the high mountains. Piero told me of his voyage to the polar regions, and
together we made great plans for the future, which covered the
whole world from the Himalaya to the mountains of Patagonia.

By the end of a week the weather had really set fair, and
the cloud formations, which had caused all our indecisions,
vanished altogether. In the afternoon we set about preparing
our sacks, and as we did so we realised that we had not enough
food for two days' climbing. We could have started all the
same, but the fates had decreed otherwise. After a brief discussion we decided to go quickly down to Chamonix for more
provisions—this, we thought, would give the weather time to
improve still further—and next day we walked down early in
the morning, did our shopping and came up again. All day
long there had not been a vestige of cloud in the sky. By nightfall our sacks were ready and we were all set to attack. We left
the hut at 2 a.m. by lantern-light and in two and a half hours
we reached the bergschrund. Here we put on our crampons
and began to climb up the steep slope at the base and to the
left of the spur of the Pointe Croz—the central spur. We
advanced slowly for the slope was hard ice and it was exhausting work cutting steps. After a hundred yards or so, to save
time we went still further to the left, to a line of smooth rocks
just protruding from the ice, on which we were able to climb
more rapidly. However we had to quit these rocks when we
reached the level of the first tower, and decided to traverse
across the slope which separated us by about fifty yards from
the spur. In order that the two of us should not both be committed, without any security, to the very hard ice of this slope,
we roped up on the full length of our 200 foot line; this would
allow me to reach rocks, where I could get a really good stance,
in one run-out.

When everything was ready I started work with my axe. I
had already covered about thirty yards when the familiar
whistle of a stone made me look round and scrutinise the upper

part of the wall to see where the danger came from. The stone hit the rock three hundred feet above me and then shot out into space. But unfortunately it had hit a block the size of a table which was lying in precarious balance just at the upper end of the funnel in which I was placed. Slowly the block heeled over and began to slide down, bringing with it a host of satellites of smaller dimensions. My head was exactly in the line of fire. For a split second I thought of letting myself slide down the slope and then swinging away out of range, but this solution was discarded as soon as thought of, for the jerk on the rope after sliding a hundred feet would have pulled Zanetti off, since he was only able to belay me over his shoulder. I saw the block gathering speed and start to bounce down the slope. I flattened myself as best I could against the ice with my arms crossed above my head in an instinctive attitude of defence. The avalanche passed by with a blast of air, miraculously leaving me untouched beneath a shower of earth and pebbles.

"Giusto, are you hurt?" Piero's agonised voice roused me.

"No," was all I replied, nor did Piero ask any more questions. Out of range of the falling stones, but linked by the rope to whatever fate might befall me, he had experienced the short-lived drama far more intensely than I had, and he was now realising that the danger was not yet over, for in my present position a second's hesitation would have spelt disaster for us both. But, as I had noticed on other occasions, in a difficult situation my reactions are perfectly lucid, I become completely detached and can move with increased safety. Automatically I clenched my teeth and began cutting steps again. Only after I had reached the rocks, twenty yards away, and had belayed myself to a solid spike did the nervous reaction set in, and for several minutes I endured a violent fit of trembling.

Just as we were skirting round the foot of the first tower to get into the couloir that leads up to the second tower, a sudden clap of thunder made us look up. This time it was no avalanche. We had been so completely absorbed by the work on the ice-slope that we had not noticed what was going on overhead. From the summit of Mont Blanc great thunder-clouds were rolling down towards the Aiguilles and the outriders had already reached and engulfed the ridge of the Jorasses. For the moment we hoped it might be a false alarm, as on the previous days, and we went on with the climb. But less than an hour later the first downpour of hail made us realise that this time it was really serious and that we had now definitely missed the favourable opportunity which had been offered us the day before.

As the storm increased in violence we beat a hasty retreat to the foot of the tower, where we took cover with our backs up against the rock beneath an overhang, put our bivouac sack over our heads and waited. It was about 10.30.

Before us lay the central portion of the wall and its great couloir, looking quite fantastic in the storm. The whole face had come to life with the snow hissing ceaselessly down the avalanche furrows, and at each clap of thunder showers of stones raked the lower part of the wall like machine-gun fire. Numb with cold, we sat looking unhappily at the steps we had cut a hundred yards away and reflecting that if we wanted to get down that was the way we should have to go. To pass the time we counted the minutes between flashes. Twelve . . . fifteen. . . . As so often happens, the storm gradually turned to settled bad weather. Snow began to fall, at first compact and frozen, then in loose wet flakes. Every moment our situation was growing worse. To go down meant taking a fifty-fifty chance with the falling stones. It might have been more prudent to wait until nightfall, when the cold, which freezes everything up and holds it in check, would put an end to the barrage. But after that, if the snow continued, should we be able to get down at all?

At 2 o'clock in the afternoon, partly to shake off the numbing effect of the piercing cold, we attempted a sortie. But after twenty yards or so, stones whistling down the face obliged us to beat a hasty retreat back to our shelter. At 3.30 we made another attempt with the same result. Then we noticed that the thunder and lightning came at longer intervals, that it was not snowing so hard, and by 5 o'clock the snow had stopped. We had had quite enough of forced inaction and, calculating that we had only just time to reach the bergschrund

North face of the Grandes Jorasses

Olan

Pic Adolphe Rey

Pic Gaspard

before dark, we fled down the murderous slope. The steps we had cut were covered with eight inches or so of fresh snow and we first had to find them and then scrape them clear. Proceeding with the utmost care we reached the rocks, but the difficulties did not diminish. Two avalanches passed close by us. Then once more we were on that very steep slope with the bergschrund beneath us. At the bottom we went back again on to the rocks overhanging the glacier. A first rappel took us to within sixty feet of the foot of these rocks. We prepared a second rappel and saw that the ends of the rope disappeared into the bergschrund. Piero went down and, by a pendulum motion, succeeded in getting across on to the lower lip. He then let go the rope and sped down the glacier stopping to keep a look-out only when he felt he was out of harm's way.

I started down in turn, but just as I set foot upon the snow there was a warning shout. It was the wall's parting shot. I took hold of the rope with both hands and threw myself into the crevasse. There was a crash of boulders on the glacier. Then I climbed up again hurriedly, pulled the rope half down, wound one end round my wrist, and raced down the glacier. The light faded and the day drew to a close as two once-proud mountaineers scuttled down the glacier, without a backward look, trailing their rope in the snow, and not even noticing the crevasses which frequently lay across their path. Night had fallen when we reached the hut by lantern-light.

At Chamonix we found Sarfatti, Piolti, Guidetti and Enriquez, and went back with them by car to Courmayeur. A few days later I returned to Chamonix with Sarfatti and Romanini to do the east face of the Grépon. This firm, splendidly sound rock restored the zest which I had lost a few days before. When I was actually on the slopes of the north face, I had sworn never to return. Now I wished myself back again, clinging to those great icy slabs. There was no hope of doing anything more that year: but it was only an encounter postponed.

Four: 1934

AT the general meeting of the Italian Academic Alpine Club at Cortina in 1934 a wish was expressed that Italy should, like other countries' clubs and societies, compete in the field of large overseas expeditions. But nothing came of the suggestion. The Academic Alpine Club, which ought to have been the moving spirit in the climbing world, was, on account of its recent re-organisation, in process of becoming a sort of museum of Italian mountaineering, and neglecting its essential role. The only thing to do was to appeal to the initiative of the Sections, but these could not aim very high, since they naturally had even fewer resources at their disposal.

In October 1933 the Turin Section, through the good offices of Dr Ferreri and of Signori Del Corno and Zanetti, made a bid to set things moving. The main difficulty was of course finance, so an ingenious plan was worked out; the expedition would be combined with a tourist cruise to the countries of South America. At first this combination did not meet with the approval of the younger climbers, but as there seemed to be no alternative, we had to welcome the idea wholeheartedly. And of course the inherent weakness of this arrangement became apparent later, for various reasons; but anyway we hoped that once the whole expedition had been somehow set in motion things would perhaps be easier.

The cruise obtained considerable support, and we were able to equip a well-matched team of mountaineers from Turin consisting of Boccalatte, Chabod, the two Ceresas, Zanetti and myself. This group was reinforced by Ghiglione, Binaghi, Brunner, and Bonacossa to whom, as president of the Academic Club, the leadership of the party was entrusted. Our preparations took up the whole winter; then on February 1 our rather

82

motley troop embarked on the s.s. *Neptunia* and sailed from Trieste.

One's first voyage aboard an ocean liner is always a peculiar experience, but for me this setting-out had a very special symbolic significance, for it was to mark the beginning of a stage in my life that I had always longed for. It was for this that I had already given up many of the things which appear to be so important in ordinary life, and for which I was ready to give up still more.

The first week at sea seemed to be all I could have wished, and I almost forgot the moral humiliation of a voyage—so very far removed from all I had set my heart on—on this floating luxury hotel. To begin with, rough seas immobilised most of the passengers, and at mealtimes there were only a bare dozen of us round the little tables. But this happy state of affairs did not last long. Once we were through the Straits of Gibraltar the weather cleared as if by magic and we enjoyed a succession of perfectly calm days. I had plenty of time to get a very clear picture of how futile life on board can be, with all those parties, and especially that business of crossing the Line. I was scarcely able to get away by myself and I even went as far as to refuse to go ashore when we put into various Brazilian ports; I was tempted only by Rio de Janeiro, one of the natural marvels of the world. With its fantastic natural setting, clearly the work of a master designer, it certainly lives up to its reputation.

We had just left Rio when we received a wireless message which was to have a considerable effect upon the outcome of our expedition. Two climbers from Buenos Aires—Matteoda and Durando, natives of Turin, the former very well known in Italian Alpine circles—had left a fortnight earlier for Tronador, a still virgin summit of northern Patagonia, and had disappeared on the mountain during a violent storm. A search-party had been unsuccessful, in spite of the Argentine Government sending a plane. Our leader, Bonacossa, sent a wire to Arlotta, our Ambassador at Buenos Aires, offering our services for a final search. So we were now obliged to abandon our original plan of action—not that I am convinced it would ever have been possible in view of the heterogeneous nature of our

party. During the following days we decided that it would be
pointless for the whole lot of us to go to Tronador, and we
unanimously agreed to split up into three parties. The first,
consisting of Bonacossa, Binaghi and myself would remain at
the service of the Embassy; the second, composed of Chabod,
Ghiglione, Stefano and Paolo Ceresa, would go to Aconcagua—
already climbed seven times, but still the highest summit of the
Andes; the third group, with Gabriele Boccalatte, Gallo, Piero
Zanetti and Brunner, would go to the Cerro Alto de Los Leones
group in the Santiago Andes.

When we docked at Montevideo more bad news awaited us
—very bad news indeed, for Bonacossa and myself. King
Albert of the Belgians, the climbing King, had been killed in a
commonplace accident on the cliffs above the river Meuse near
Brussels. His love of climbing, the inspiration of his whole life,
had been his undoing. He used to snatch brief respite from the
heavy cares of State by training climbs on these rocks, which
kept him fit for his holidays in the Alps. Our arrival at Buenos
Aires was overshadowed by these two catastrophes; further,
we had to undergo a lot of unwelcome publicity as a result
of the cruise, and this considerably slowed down our preparations. At last we got away in three groups as arranged:
the others were bound for Mendoza, and ourselves for San
Carlos de Bariloche, after we had attended a private lunch
given by our Ambassador, at which we made the necessary
arrangements for the search for Matteoda and Durando. The
train journey across the Pampas to Los Junos was horribly
dusty and lasted two days and two nights; for the final lap
to Bariloche we travelled by car.

Beyond the Pampas we came to the region of the great
Argentine lakes at the northern extremity of Patagonia—a district of great natural beauty, which, though little frequented
by tourists, had already begun to attract attention and to be
visited by the initiated. Its main feature is its chain of lakes,
narrow and enclosed like winding inland fjords, but with banks
covered in luxuriant vegetation. From Bariloche we continued
our journey, partly by van, partly on a small steamer, until
we came to the edge of the forest beyond which rose Tronador,

and here we rearranged our baggage for the tedious march
through the forest. With some difficulty we succeeded in estab-
lishing our base camp near the edge of the great glaciers. But
nothing would persuade the local porters to go any further, for
they were horribly frightened by the glaciers, even when these
were flat and uncrevassed. However, from this point the big
northern glacier of Tronador was easily within reach. Our
upper camp site was the same as that used by Matteoda and
Durando.

On the first day two great condors paid us a visit, flying in
wide circles around the tents. One of them alighted about
thirty yards away, but once they had made sure we were living
creatures and not carrion they made off. I was very sorry that
I had no gun at hand, and Bonacossa made fun of me by depict-
ing my return with a trophy ten foot across and certain election
to the Presidency of my local sporting club. But we had no
time to play at Tartarin and my old hunting instincts were soon
submerged by more pressing concerns.

For two days we were confined to camp by bad weather. On
the third we were able to begin the search, but though we
scrutinised the great glaciers through our glasses from many
different observation points, we could discover no signs of anyone—either living or dead. Slowly the new landscape became
familiar. The mountains of this region do not form a real
chain, but stick out here and there among the lakes and forests.
The still unclimbed Puntiagudo looks like a newly sharpened
pencil, so pointed and regular is its volcanic cone. The Osorno,
further away, has the classic shape of a volcano with a round
truncated cone. We pushed on up to the col separating the
two summits of Tronador and climbed the Chilean peak which
we named Picco Matteoda in memory of the missing climber.
Bonacossa then returned quickly to inform the Ambassador
in Buenos Aires of the result of our search, while Binaghi and
I struck camp and followed on down the valley.

We joined up again with Bonacossa and took the train on the
Chilean line to Santiago where we found Zanetti's party. After
a few days in Santiago, where we were given an extremely
cordial welcome by the Italian residents, the whole party left

for the central Andes where we hoped to climb Marmolejo at the head of the Engarda valley. But many days of bad weather with heavy falls of snow put an end to this plan. Time was getting short and the day was approaching when we should have to start back. According to the programme the return journey was to be made aboard the *Virgilio* via the Panama Canal back to the Atlantic. But I could not resign myself to the idea of returning with such pitiable results after having come so far. I found a kindred spirit in Binaghi, and after various calculations we decided to remain until the end of the season. Opposite Marmolejo is a fine unnamed peak, bold in outline and certainly over 16,000 feet high, which we chose as our next objective. However, since fresh snow precluded an immediate attack we left one tent with our equipment and returned to Santiago with the others. Here we found Chabod's party, which had climbed the Cerro Querno and Aconcagua.

On March 21 Binaghi and I said goodbye to our friends who were making the return voyage to Italy on the *Virgilio*. After returning to the mountains by car we once again mounted the little Chilean ponies and made our way slowly towards the high Engarda valley. We were accompanied by an Italian, Mattei, as well as by the two usual *arrieros*, the local muleteers and guides, with loaded mules.

The new snow which had forced us to retreat when we were at the upper Marmolejo camp a few days before, had almost disappeared lower down, but it still lay above 15,000 feet, clinging to the strange formations known as penitentes, or plastered to the rocks on south faces. As the mules ambled along we anxiously examined conditions on the mountain, since on these depended the success or failure of the attempt we had decided to make upon the unnamed peak. Unlike most of these mountains, which are rounded, it rises from the ridge of the Cortateras, the highest point in the group, in a slender, bold and rocky pyramid overlooking steep chaotic glaciers.

If conditions were bad the difficulties would be greatly increased, and so, punctuating our speculations upon the possibilities and probabilities of an ascent with vigorous tugs at our horses' reins, we slowly made our way to the upper Engarda plateau where, at about 10,500 feet, we had left our base camp equipment. We found the tent and the cases of provisions intact. We sorted out our equipment, made our preparations for the higher camp and, since we should not have far to go, we fixed our departure for 10 a.m. the following morning.

The next day, March 22, we loaded a couple of cases on to one of the mules and set out for the head of the valley. After much zig-zagging about on the ups and downs of the moraine which formed the bed of the valley, we succeeded in getting on to the glacier descending from the col beneath our peak. Here, at 12,500 feet, we established our last camp. Mattei, who had come with us, took some photographs and then accompanied the *arriero* back to base camp. We soon withdrew into the tent, for, once the sun had disappeared, the cold outside became intense. But before shutting ourselves in we noticed that a fish-shaped cloud had formed over the summit of Marmolejo—a portent which in Italy would not have been considered favourable. The next day we were to learn that in this respect a change of country made no difference.

The following morning when we left the tent to go up on to the glacier it was 7 a.m.—rather late, but the intense cold had deterred us from putting our noses out any earlier. We crossed the glacier, which was level for a hundred yards or so before it rose steeply. As soon as we began to climb we found that the snow had not consolidated as we had thought, but had remained light and powdery and, as everyone knows, that is not at all pleasant on a snow climb. We immediately put on our crampons and continued with caution. Meanwhile the wind blew up great banks of cloud from the north-west: evidently the weather was going to break. But we hoped for a bit of luck and did not consider turning back. The penitentes were quite small here—about twelve to eighteen inches and completely snow-covered. It was not long before we met the first difficulties. The way was barred by huge crevasses extending right across the glacier and at each of these we were forced to make a long détour to find crossing-places which were mostly very awkward. Half-way up the glacier we came to a gigantic crevasse twenty to thirty yards wide, and we had considerable difficulty before we eventually succeeded in crossing it over on the right. To begin with we had to climb down into it, cutting steps in bare ice; we went along it for a few yards and then discovered a sort of track varying from four to twelve inches in width and about thirty yards long, which led to the upper lip of the crevasse. We got on to it low down by forcing a way up a seven-foot wall of vertical ice. Having overcome this obstacle with some difficulty we continued to plod up through the penitentes sinking up to our calves in the snow which became progressively deeper as we gained height.

Beneath the slope leading up to the col the glacier flattened out to end on the right in a rounded hog's back. At the foot of the slope was a crevasse whose formation resembled that of an ordinary bergschrund, and above it the angle of the slope was extremely steep—more than 50°. Here the penitentes were very high—on an average about seven feet—so that it was a real climb to get over them and this, combined with the powdery snow which had accumulated in between, made it all a most awkward performance. This was the hardest part and progress was very slow indeed. Sometimes it seemed almost as though we were climbing on granite slabs for we had to cling with our hands to the crests of the penitentes, and these were extremely thin, with filigree edges which had first to be broken away to leave something more solid; sometimes we had to back-and-knee, as though we were climbing a chimney, in between two penitentes of sheer ice.

At 2.30, after seven hours exhausting climbing, we reached the col at about 15,800 feet. The weather had now turned definitely bad. The sky was overcast, the wind howled over the ridge, and a scattering of small hailstones began to fall. But we were quite close to the summit and had no intention of giving up, not even at the price of an improvised bivouac which would now be inevitable if we went on. We quickly ate some food and at 3 p.m. started up the ridge. The climbing was not really hard, and the rock on these mountains might be termed reasonably good. We tried to turn the gendarmes on the east, and to avoid the crest of the ridge as far as possible, for the wind there was so violent as to constitute a major obstacle. On the few pitches that we could not circumvent, we hugged the rock like limpets, keeping the whole length of our bodies in contact with it so as not to be blown off.

We reached the summit at 4.30 and did not wait long. We built a cairn, in which we left the new name of the peak, the Cerro Campione d'Italia, and started down; in an hour we were back at the col. We chose a bivouac site ten yards or so below the ridge where it was slightly sheltered: there was no question of going down any lower on account of the penitentes. We made a little hollow, built a circular wall, got into our feather-weight bivouac-sack and huddled together. The sun was setting and, even though the weather was getting worse, it did just put in an appearance to wish us good night. Suddenly, as it sank, it broke through the circle of clouds and for a few minutes we beheld a fantastic scene. The clouds massed all around us, and the contrasting colours, gave an impression of power such as I had never before witnessed. We remained spellbound, forgetting all about the cold and the bivouac, while the mist still floated beneath us, cutting us off completely from the world below. In the sky the mass of cloud settled into alternate layers, each tinged half blood-red, half a terrifying black. Opposite us Marmolejo appeared and disappeared in wildly swirling mist and cloud, sometimes showing through a golden veil, sometimes with its glaciers glowing flame-red, sometimes plumed with menacing vapours that alternately hid its walls, or parted to reveal them. With its flames and swirling shadows, it might have been a scene from Dante's Inferno. It lasted a few minutes, then night closed in, the fantastic play of colours faded, and everything became grey and flat. The mist rose up and mingled with the clouds, and finally everything was wrapped in darkness. The bivouac had begun. Binaghi ushered it in with an old peasant proverb, "*Quant ul su 'al turna indrée ghèm l'acqua ai pée*"—When the sun goes backwards [i.e. behind a cloud] we shall have water underfoot. A proverb which proved correct.

Over our heads we put a small cape of waterproofed silk and, huddling close together, ironically wished each other good night. We could not sleep, we could not move. All we could

do was to think. To think of many things: of our homes, of
our own far-distant country where the sun would now be
shining, of the happy peaceful people warm and snug in their
houses.

Then the first shiver of cold ran right down our spines, and
spread to our limbs, followed by the second, and the third . . .
and so on for twelve long hours. The trend of one's thoughts
changed: first one worried about the left foot, for it seemed to
have gone numb. Would it still be functioning tomorrow?
Then, as though this were not enough, the weather took a hand.
At 8 p.m. snow began to fall, at first frozen and mixed with little
hailstones, then in a fine powder. The wind sent it eddying
round and round and against this our shelter was of precious
little use. It got under the cape, slipped down our necks, into
our noses, into the bivouac-sack—everywhere. At each squall
we huddled closer together. Our teeth danced a devilish taran-
tella which we were powerless to stop. Every half-hour we had
to shake off the snow which threatened to bury us. Around us
it piled up alarmingly: What about tomorrow? Should we be
able to get down, or was this to be the end of us—transformed
into ice-mummies for all eternity? Sometimes we longed to give
up and let ourselves go, to shut our eyes and sink once and for
all into oblivion, letting the snow enshroud us softly, warmly.
How good it would be not to feel the pain in that foot any more,
nor the biting cold in one's limbs, nor the damp which per-
meated us through and through. . . . But our determination
reasserted itself, tautening every nerve; we stared wide-eyed
into the dark. I dreamed of the sun, the blazing sun. The sun
flooding a shining beach with a group of girls holding hands,
dancing and singing. Dancing—yes, but the dance was of the
whirling snow-flakes which stifled our breathing for seconds at
a time. And so it went on for hours, without respite.

Morning found us in rather poor fettle. The weather was the
same as it had been during the night. Nearly thirty inches of
snow had fallen and visibility was down to twenty yards. The
moment we put our noses outside the shelter of our wall the
wind choked us. Get down, though, we must. With this idea
firmly fixed in our heads, we shook off the last of the snow, got

out of our bivouac sack, packed our rucksacks and plunged into the blizzard. The first hundred yards were absolutely desperate. We had to make a terrific effort just to breathe. We couldn't tell where we were going and it seemed as though we, the penitentes and the mountain were all going round and round in a mad whirl. It was no longer a descent, but a series of falls from one penitente to the next in the mass of snow which had piled up during the night. We went straight ahead, blindly, floundering in small avalanches that slid down the gullies between these strange formations. Once I went headlong and became completely submerged in the snow. I fell with my axe beneath me and the force of my fall drove the point into my right thigh. As soon as I could stand up I pulled it out of the wound. I was very much afraid that I should no longer be able to walk, but I found I could bear up all right, and although blood was running freely down my leg my one thought was to get on. We went down another fifty yards and then, when we came to a place where the wind was slightly less violent, we stopped a moment to recover our breath. But even then I was not able to examine my injury, for we could neither take off our gloves—our fingers would have frozen instantly—nor could we undo our clothes, which had been soaked through during the night so that we were encased from head to foot in ice. Anyway, just looking at the wound wouldn't have done any good, and once I discovered that I could move freely, I knew that the injury was only a flesh wound, and there was nothing to do but go on down. While we were on the steep parts, it wasn't too bad, but the worst began after we had crossed the first large crevasse or bergschrund and were down on the glacier below. Here all the snow blown off the ridges had accumulated and in some places there were drifts over six feet deep. As we went forward we made a regular trench in the snow; we sank in up to our waists and, although the slope was in our favour, we had to relieve one another at trail-breaking every fifty yards.

Crossing the very large crevasse was particularly difficult and dangerous, for the upper slope threatened to avalanche at any moment and sweep us down to the bottom of the chasm. However, we succeeded in getting across all right, and on we went, walking like a couple of robots, through a sea of snow. Our legs would scarcely carry us—determination alone kept us going and we longed only to lie down in the snow. But we knew we must keep moving, for if once we stopped we should never start again.

It was 4 p.m. when we reached the upper camp, where the *arriero*, good fellow, was awaiting us. In spite of the snow he had come up, according to plan, to fetch the tent. He had been much alarmed not to find us there, and said he had given us up for lost. Then, with the air of a conjurer, he produced a bottle of Cinzano which the good Mattei had sent to cheer us up. We did not wait to be asked twice but grabbed it in the most undignified manner. After we had packed up the tent we trudged back to base camp which we reached as dark was falling. The tents were half buried in snow, but inside we found a little of the warmth our bodies craved. Cook, an engineer, with whom we had been going to climb Marmolejo, had come up to this camp, but with the quantity of fresh snow this plan was now out of the question. Two days later we all went down to Santiago.

After the trials and tribulations of Cerro Campione d'Italia, we stayed several days at Santiago to recuperate. My thigh injury had healed rapidly, and now we hesitated between the two climbs on our programme. The Cerro Alto de Los Leones was certainly the more tempting, but on account of the recent heavy snow-fall we decided to fall back on the unnamed Cerro we had spotted between Cerros Alto and Plomo, and which was easily visible from the Plaza Italia at Santiago. Moreover the route we should be attempting on this peak lay up a ridge facing north and consequently exposed to the sun, where the snow would not lie for long. Mondini, who was in Rio Blanco, told us over the telephone that conditions in the Leones were bad, and this finally put an end to our hesitation and confirmed us in our decision.

On March 30 we travelled in a fast lorry to Coral Quemado where we spent the night at the hut belonging to the Ski Club of Chile. On the morning of the 31st we set out on horseback and with loaded mules for the Casa de Piedra de Carvajal, an

immense boulder situated at the head of an interminable valley
at about 10,500 feet; we arrived just in time to pitch our tents
in the fading light of a grey and misty day. We had with us
Mattei, a fellow-countryman, and an enterprising young Scot
called Buchanan, a member of the Ski Club.

On April 1 we realised that the bag containing the bundle
of tents for the upper camp had been left behind at Coral
Quemado. We sent the *arriero* back to fetch them, but set off
ourselves all the same; taking a large tent we went in search of
a site for the higher camp. At 2 p.m. we found one at about
13,000 feet, but a sudden snowstorm forced us to return to our
base camp with all the equipment. On April 2 the weather
cleared and a hot sun rapidly melted the snow. That evening,
seeing that the small tents had still not arrived and fearing that
the changeable weather might play us false again, we decided
to leave by night and do without the upper camp that had
originally been planned.

We realised that this decision would involve a special effort;
but we were not to regret it for it enabled us to carry out our
ascent successfully through taking advantage of the only two
fine days. We arranged with Mattei that as soon as the tents
arrived he would bring them up to the agreed site at 13,000 feet
so that on the descent we should have shelter nearer at hand.
On April 3 we left base camp at 3 a.m. with Buchanan, who
was to come with us as far as the beginning of the climb. The
full moon was a great help and we moved quickly, more particularly as the intense cold gave us no incentive to dally.

We followed exactly the same route we had taken on April 1.
On the upper moraines we were met by icy gusts of wind, and
at 6.30 we came to the foot of the buttress up which we intended to climb and which we thought would bring us out on
to the ridge. We got on to this buttress at a saddle, after climbing up a snow slope for about 300 feet, and then continued up
for a while, but were finally obliged to skirt round some earth
towers with bits of rock embedded in them—the bases of nearly
all these mountains are formed of curious conglomerates. In
doing this we lost height and came to a sort of scoop lying
between the real north ridge and our buttress. This broad

couloir was furrowed by a number of stone shoots and we made for the easiest looking of them.

As we climbed up, the slope steepened. In the lower part the scree had been loose and shifting, but higher up it was embedded in a cement of ice and formed an extremely hard reinforced concrete on which we could get no purchase with our nails. We had to use our axes to cut steps. But it was not at all like cutting steps in ice, for this stony conglomerate split in all directions beneath the axe. The slope was at an angle of nearly 50° and in consequence the ascent was slow and very difficult. To make matters worse, close up beneath the ridge the terrain became even more complex. The couloir fanned out, ending in a number of extremely friable little rock walls—if one could call it rock! After every rope-length we anxiously sought a way out. There was no question of attacking the wall direct. Once again we climbed up for a hundred feet, this time on a layer of powder snow which made things still more treacherous; then over on our right there appeared a possible way out—a shallow groove in the wall by which we could escape. It was a vein of a whitish mineral about four inches wide and about fifty feet long, also covered with ice. Cutting steps which crumbled away and endeavouring to make ourselves as light as possible for fear that everything should slide from under our feet, we succeeded in slowly forcing a way and at last emerged into sunlight. Another couple of rope-lengths and we set foot upon the ridge at about 16,500 feet.

It was 11.30 and we had been going for eight hours without being able to make a halt. We found a spot sheltered from the wind on the east side behind a projecting bit of rock and stopped for a few minutes to bask in the sun, for we were numb with cold after our gloomy couloir. At the same time we examined the ridge. We could not see very much of it for it was long and there were many gendarmes, but it did not look too difficult. What worried us more was the quality of the rock; here, although it was rock all right—no longer earth as we had found lower down—it was little better than a pile of tottering blocks.

At 11.45 we began to climb. For the most part we had to

remain on the crest of the ridge, and when sometimes we were
forced off it we climbed on the eastern flank, for on the west
the wall fell away steeply for more than three thousand feet.
There were really no pitches of any very great technical difficulty, it was more a question of acrobatics on boulders poised
in uncertain balance on airy little crests overhanging precipices on either side, or upon pinnacles which remained upright
only by a miracle.

. In this way we covered half the length of the ridge. Ahead
of us a cluster of spiky gendarmes seemed firmly to bar the way,
but we prepared to attack them with a will, convinced that we
should find the summit immediately on the far side. The first
gendarme yielded fairly easily, but it was joined to the second
by a knife-edged ridge which gave us considerable trouble. The
second gendarme was not easy either, for we had to pull away
at least five holds for every one that was sound. We surmounted
this obstacle without mishap, but a disagreeable surprise was in
store for us; instead of our coveted peak, a secondary summit
lay before us on the far side of a gap some 150 feet deep. We
climbed quickly down into it. It was now 1.30, and though we
were pressed for time, we stopped for something to eat as the
summit was still far off. Meanwhile a few clouds appeared in
the sky and a great bank of mist began to rise up from below.
The ridge ran level for some way and was rather dull, then we
came to the wall of the secondary summit. Here the rock was
firmer and we found a few pitches of some style. We were
breathless from the height when we reached the top; quickly
we glanced at what lay ahead, and were overjoyed to see the
real summit, easy, rounded and covered with scree. Summoning all our energy we set off as fast as we could run, or so it
seemed to us! A few more yards and—the monotonous whistling of the wind was broken by a torrent of unedifying invective.
It was not the summit; this lay a good distance further on.
Half an hour, we reckoned.

We sat down, utterly disgusted. The mist rose in swirling
eddies and the wind blew violently. We left our sacks and
plodded on, no longer with any of our former enthusiasm, but
dazed and quite convinced that the summit was bewitched and

would retreat as fast as we advanced. Doggedly at first, then
once again increasing our pace towards the end, we really did
arrive on the summit this time. On the far side the ridge
dropped away; there was nothing above us. Our aneroid registered 17,700 feet and our watches 3.30. The mist surged up
and swirled all round us, but after a few minutes the wind
dispersed it and the immense panorama of the Central Andes
spread out before us from the Mercedario to the Cumbre, beyond which towered Aconcagua; then once more the mist blew
up in violent gusts. We built a cairn, the tangible sign of our
victory, leaving in it a metal box containing our flag and a
christening card with the name Cerro Littoria. Then we ran
back to our sacks. It would have taken too long to return down
the ridge, and we were lucky to find a steep snow couloir on the
east-north-east face; we embarked upon this resolutely in spite
of signs of frequent stone-falls, for it provided a quick way down
and enabled us to avoid an otherwise certain bivouac. At the
foot we came to the glacier and, crossing its upper portion to
the left, bade a last farewell to the penitentes.

At 6.30 we came to the col to the north of the ridge up which
we had climbed and there we stopped a while to watch the
flaming sunset. Then, while the great orb sank slowly into
the distant Pacific, leaving a long streak of brightness on the
horizon, we ran headlong down the easy névé. It was pitch dark
when we came to the first moraines, but we did not want to
wait for the moon which would not rise till later, so we continued by lantern-light among enormous heaps of boulders
until a distant voice replied to our shouts: it was Mattei who
had come up to about 13,000 feet to pitch the tent. He made
signals to us by burning newspapers which enabled us to reach
the camp without mishap.

After a good night we packed up the tents on April 4 and
went down to our base camp. Here we found Buchanan and
the son of the *arriero*, a youth of fourteen, both looking very
anxious. The first evening, the *arriero* had accompanied Mattei
up to the higher camp, taking a mule; afterwards he had gone
off to look for two of the mules which had broken their tether-
ing ropes and gone back down the valley in search of better

grazing. The two young fellows had thus been left alone, and
that evening, by the fire on which they were grilling slices of
kid, the boy had unburdened himself of thoughts which must
have been troubling him a lot. He told a story, heard at Coral
Quemado a few years back, about how the Casa de Piedra de
Carvajal was used as a hiding-place by a band of brigands who
stripped travellers coming up the valley and sent them back
naked as the day they were born. Then one day these char-
acters had gone over one of the frontier passes and disappeared
into the Argentine pampas. Suppose they were to return?
And the two had got so worked up by the story that it ended
in their putting out the fire and instead of getting into their
downy sleeping-bags in the tents, they had spent the night on
top of the great boulder from which the place takes its name.

The following day they were half convinced that the bandits
had made a reconnaissance in preparation for an attack the
next night, when they would go off with our clothes, and they
had anxiously awaited our return. Now the son of the *arriero*
hinted strongly that really the best thing would be to pack up
the tents and go off down the valley. Naturally this met with
loud guffaws on our part and we teased them for having let
themselves be so frightened. Well pleased with our own success
and our first ascent, all afternoon we continued to make jokes
at their expense. Towards evening the *arriero* returned on
horse-back towing the truant mules behind him.

After a supper of the usual *cazuela*, or stew, and the usual kid
roasted under the stones, we gathered round the fire, throwing
on all the reserves of wood we had brought up from below since
we would be going down the next day. Under the influence of
Buchanan, who was in love and kept sighing for the girl he had
left behind him for a few days, Gino started on his repertory of
romantic songs. After a bit, seeing that our young friend was
in danger of giving way to his emotions, I had an idea for an
appropriate practical joke. I withdrew a little into the shadow
and without letting myself be seen I threw a stone so that it fell
between the tents. At this noise everyone jumped up with one
thought: the brigands! Of course I made haste to explain the
mystery, but my joke had so disturbed the apparently smooth

waters that when we retired to our tents—the four of us in the bigger one and the *arriero* and his son in the other a little way off—we took with us our only effective weapons: the ice-axes!

At about 1 o'clock I woke with a start. The moon was already high in the sky and clearly illuminated the interior of the tent. I thought I heard a dragging footstep at regular intervals. I strained my ears to listen: the noise was repeated. I sat up to hear better and at the same moment Mattei did so too. He had heard what I had. We woke Buchanan and Binaghi and all listened together: we agreed that it was undoubtedly someone walking. We decided therefore to open the tent flap quietly, then to rush out, making as much noise as possible so as at any rate to frighten our adversary. At the agreed signal we leaped out brandishing our axes and howling like savages. If the *arriero* and his son, who had been sleeping peacefully in the other tent close by, did not die of heart failure, it showed that, for all their fear, they hadn't got weak hearts. Outside, the big boulders and the dark forms of the mules made a peaceful scene in the moonlight. We took a look round. Nothing. We returned to the tents. The noise began again. But it seemed more like a rustling now. We went in the direction of the noise and there between two boulders we found a crumpled newspaper which the draught was blowing rhythmically backwards and forwards. To what absurd lengths imagination can lead one! We went back into the tent to meditate upon our childishness.

On April 5 we struck camp, said a last "goodbye" to the Andes and started on our way down. After stopping a few days in Santiago, we went by car to Mendoza and then by train to Buenos Aires. On April 15 we embarked aboard the *Augustus*, bound for Italy.

Five: 1934

AT the beginning of the 1934 season I spent a few days in the Dolomites with Colonnetti. Meanwhile Chabod, with whom I had arranged to climb that year in the Mont Blanc district, went off to wait for me at Courmayeur.

We paid a brief visit to the Tre Cime di Lavaredo, and then went to the Civetta group where we made the second ascent of the Campanile di Brabante. This curious needle which leans up against the south bastion of the great wall interested me from a technical point of view because of its really exceptional first pitch, which I managed to climb successfully without artificial aids, using only the first piton for a belay. Coming down there is an amusing free rappel.

When I returned to Turin I found a card from Chabod begging me to go to Courmayeur as he was all alone there and felt that he was gently falling a victim to the pleasures of the valley. I immediately sent off a wire with two words only: "Resist, coming". I stopped just long enough to send on my things and get fresh equipment, and then set off for Courmayeur. Chabod gave me the latest news of an attempt by Charlet and Gréloz on the north face of the Grandes Jorasses following the route that Zanetti and I had attempted in 1933. The great French guide had got as far as the band of slabs which was the unknown element of the climb.

At the end of July we crossed the Col du Géant to the Leschaux hut. Since our stay there the year before it had been enlarged and modernised; there was even a guardian who served meals. So we were no longer to be alone in our glory this year, but surrounded by a continual influx of mountaineers.

The great wall had now become a magnet which drew the climbers of five nationalities. The guardian told us that already there had been two attempts that season besides Charlet's, by Lambert and Loulou Boulaz, and by Steinauer and Martin Meier. On our arrival we had the pleasure of seeing two little black dots pinpricked in the great central couloir. These were Peters and Haringer who had attacked that night and were now obviously in difficulty, judging by the extreme slowness of their movements. There were also three Austrians camping not far from the hut, who had certainly not come that far just to sightsee. Apparently there were other parties from Munich in Chamonix, among them Franz Schmid, one of the conquerors of the north face of the Matterhorn. So we were now in the acute stage of the race for the Grandes Jorasses, and I remembered a prophetic article published in a French journal[1] in which the author described the day when the great glacier would be turned into an enclosure with a turnstile for spectators and, perched up on the Drus to get a good view of the final, a gang of gate-crashers. . . . After all the mountains belong to everyone; there was nothing we could do but make the best of it and set out that same night.

After a meal we went and lay down on the bunks to rest. Then suddenly, as I was dozing, I heard someone come in; I got up to see who it was and recognised Charlet. So I woke Chabod and we went down to have a few words with him. After some conversational sparring, during which we tried not to disclose our real intentions, it finally came out that we should all find ourselves together on the wall the next morning —naturally without any serious intentions! Meanwhile the Germans had given up trying to ascend the couloir and had made a long traverse across to the right-hand spur. We lost sight of them on the rocks, and they bivouacked somewhere below the tower.

At 1 a.m. we were ready to leave the hut and this time we were favoured by a brilliant full moon. Charlet and Belin, another Chamonix guide, left shortly after and, going at Charlet's usual speed, they caught us up and forged ahead. We

[1] By Etienne Bruhl, illustrated by Samivel, in *Alpinisme*, 1930. [*Translators' Note.*]

didn't let ourselves be tempted into trying to keep up with them for this would have meant arriving exhausted at the bergschrund. And we reflected, too, that they would have to cut up the slope and that it would be easier for us to catch up with them there. Not until we were in shadow close under the wall, and could no longer pick out the figures of the two guides ahead, did we have to force our pace in order to see the point at which they had attacked it, and so waste no time looking for their tracks. Chabod crossed the bergschrund about 200 feet behind the two French guides. It was still dark and we were in deep shadow and were not even able to take advantage of the moonlight. Charlet was moving fast, going straight up; we were bombarded with ice-chips sent flying by his axe, which was most unpleasant since they were coming from some distance above. Once up the slope, which was ice in the upper part, we entered the little couloir between the two towers and the wall. At this moment a few stones began to come down. There were now two parties above us and we had to move with extreme caution if we wished to avoid being hit. We heard voices below and saw that a party of three had crossed the bergschrund and begun to climb up—no doubt the Austrians whose camp we had seen. So now we were nine, representing four nations, and Samivel's prophecy was coming true. Only the gate-crashers on the Drus were lacking.

While we were continuing up the snow, avoiding the rocks, a few stones fell close to Chabod and he was hit by one on the arm and nearly lost his balance. At the little col by the first tower we stopped a while to let the party we could see ahead of us (not Charlet, who was already higher, but the Germans who had bivouacked here) finish a difficult pitch in the little couloir, then we started again. While we were climbing this pitch ourselves I heard Renato asking someone a question. It was Charlet, coming down as rapidly as he had gone up, and his answer came in no uncertain terms: "Nothing doing, it's all ice." We gave him a friendly word and went on.

On the second tower we stopped in the sun to eat and at the same time examined the wall above. The two Germans were about 150 feet higher up, going extremely slowly and putting in pitons. Charlet's words were beginning to take effect. As a Western Alps specialist, Renato was under the powerful influence of the myth of the infallibility of local guides. He was convinced that if Armand turned back it meant that the verglas higher up would really make the climb impossible. I insisted that we should at least go up as far as the band of snow which is the key to the climb. We decided to leave our crampons and continue.

We soon caught up with the German party whose leader had abandoned the rock and gone back to the ice slope, traversing to the right. Chabod shouted a greeting across to them, but they appeared not to notice our presence, and did not even reply. It was impossible for us to get past them at this point, for the pitch could not be avoided and so once again we stopped. This time the hold-up proved definitely fatal.

We had been getting into our stride again and if we had been able to go straight ahead, we might perhaps have regained our lost confidence. But this hanging about and waiting had once more sapped our determination. I would have liked to go as far as the famous barrier of slabs so as to see at close quarters the real possibilities of finding a way through. But Chabod pointed out that this would mean bivouacking on the descent—a pretty sound argument. Nevertheless I tried to force the issue and kept on the heels of the second German, but then the leader suddenly began to climb down. Were they also intending to give up? This was the last blow to our wavering determination. Time was getting on and these untoward happenings had already made it likely we should have to bivouac in any case, even if we turned back at once. So we made up our minds and arranged the first rappel.

When we reached the little col by the second tower we looked up and saw that the Germans were continuing the ascent, so it wasn't long before we began to regret having given up. However the die was cast and there was nothing for it but to go on down. Below us, on the col by the first tower, the three members of the last party had stopped. We couldn't understand why they were still there; maybe they had thought better of continuing the climb. Anyway we didn't suppose they intended to settle there for the duration.

We descended the great bastion between the two towers by a long hundred-foot rappel, not following the route we had taken on the way up, but keeping to the crest of the rib. Then, try as we would, we could not get the rope down. This is an old story, but in our position it was particularly disagreeable. Hearing my bad-tempered comments, Chabod helpfully suggested: "It's quite simple! Put on your espadrilles, climb up and unhook it!" Very simple indeed it sounded, but it was another matter to do it. I changed my boots, took hold of the rope and hauled myself up the overhang hand over hand. With very great difficulty I succeeded in getting on to a narrow flake twenty-five feet up where I installed myself, and then after considerable effort I was fortunately able to get the rope to run and all was ready to pull it right down. But I had to get down myself and to do so I should have to rappel from where I was. In my haste to get up I had forgotten to take the necessary hammer and pitons which one usually stows away in one's sack before one starts to rappel; and now I had to get Chabod to send the things up on the rope in the usual way. Now for the big moment! I put in a piton, threaded a piece of line and before knotting it looped it round the rope I was about to pull down. In this way when the end of the rope came whistling down from above, the rappel would automatically be in position for me to descend.

By the time I was through with "operation rappel", directed from a most precarious position, I had just about had enough. I joined Chabod and we resumed the descent down to the three climbers waiting below. Scarcely had we reached them when they asked us politely, in French, where we were going. This question put us in high good humour, and Chabod replied hilariously that for the time being our intention was to get back to the hut before nightfall. So then they said that if we really didn't mind they would come with us. We saw what they were driving at, and told them to follow us. We knew that Charlet had discovered a way down from the little col by a couloir facing the Périades—thus avoiding the deadly initial

slope which the year before had been the scene of an adventure
I would not easily forget. We now made our way down this
couloir, followed by the Austrians.

It was a tiresome descent and because of the risk of sending
stones down on to each other we had to wait at every exposed
pitch; this and the fact that the ropes were now wet and
would not run through the rappel loops slowed us up. To save
time we used all the ropes available: while the whole party
were going down on two of the ropes I got the other two in
position. Arranging the last rappel above the bergschrund I
found extremely disagreeable. The previous rappel had taken
me to the bottom of the rock buttress and in the darkness—
night had long since fallen—I could see a vertical wall of ice
disappearing beneath my feet into the even blacker gloom of
the bergschrund. I fastened myself to the rappel rope and cut a
large platform at the foot of the rocks, and there I set about
putting in a piton. I must admit that the drop underneath
held a strange fascination for me. Reluctantly I undid myself
from the rope, for it was imperative that the others should
begin to descend, but I felt uneasy during the whole operation.
Finally I sent the second rope shooting out into space and the
two ends disappeared into the bergschrund. To get a footing
on the glacier it was necessary to make a pendulum swing
across. Praying for good luck I let myself slide down into the
dark. The pendulum was a hundred per cent successful and I
landed on the lower lip.

Always, at the end of a day of bitter struggle, when I succeed
in setting foot on *terra firma*—even if, as in the present case,
it consists of a not easily accessible glacier—I feel at once as
though a great weight has been lifted from me, just as one feels
on waking from a nightmare; and this time the pleasure was
even greater than usual.

My thoughts were interrupted by the arrival of the others
who were guided by the light of the lantern I had lit; when the
last man of the second party was almost down, Chabod and I,
who were beginning to get numb with cold, started back to the
hut.

The sky was full of stars, but the snow was unaccountably

soft. Was the weather about to change? If so, Peters and Haringer, who were bivouacking for the second night, would not
be very happy next day. In fact, the following morning when
we got up from our bunks after a good night's rest and went
outside, we found an icy rain falling—higher up it would be
snowing—and the whole wall was wrapped in cloud. In the
afternoon we decided to return to Courmayeur, and went
across to the Requin hut where we spent the night.

Tragedy had overtaken Peters and Haringer. They were
blocked high up by the snow, and as they were coming down
Haringer slipped on the ice at the bottom of a rappel and fell
more than 1,500 feet to the glacier below. Peters continued
the descent alone with the vision continually before him of his
friend lying battered at the foot of the wall. It took him another
two days to reach the bottom, so that he had been on the face
for five days and four nights consecutively.

After a few days' rest in Courmayeur we made our way once
more up to the Torino hut on the Col du Géant. The weather
was very changeable, half a day of sunshine alternating with
half a day of snow; in the fine intervals we went out on skis.
We had no very definite objective in mind as yet. One day we
made tracks up to the Col de la Fourche de la Brenva, but by
next day they had disappeared. And thus it was that our
impatience at this forced inactivity drove us on to conceive of
an enterprise which, in the prevailing conditions, promised
such objective dangers as to make it seem almost hopeless.

Not far from the hut lies the east face of Mont Blanc du
Tacul. We had admired it many a time from many different
viewpoints and our gaze had often lingered on it as we searched
for a possible route on the gigantic central pillar of rock whose
sheer buttresses fall three thousand feet and more to the Vallée
Blanche. On the left Antoldi, Boccalatte, Chabod, Gallo and
Ghiglione had already climbed part of the way up a couloir
leading to the Brèche de l'Isolée and then continued up a rock
rib. On the right a party consisting of De Filippi, Ghiglione
and Ravelli had tried up another vertiginous couloir, which
they had been forced to abandon for an extremely exposed

traverse to the right, after which they continued up rocks leading to the ridge. The problem of the ice-slope leading direct to the summit still remained unsolved—a highly attractive undertaking, no doubt, but excessively dangerous. The first essential was to convince ourselves of the feasibility of the climb. If you are checkmated on rock you can always make an elegant retreat by rappelling. On ice it is never pleasant to go down. We set off, therefore, on the usual reconnaissance.

In its upper portion this couloir ends in a formidable wall of ice, vertical and unclimbable, which drops from the ridge and bars all possibility of an exit over a distance of about 200 yards. Only on the left did the slope appear to circumvent the obstacle and run up to the snow ridge near the east summit. But distance and perspective prevented our making a real estimate and merely increased our uncertainty. We realised that we could not form an opinion in advance but would have to come to a decision on the spot, and trust to luck that we should find the key to the wall of séracs. In other respects the climb seemed to be in good condition, in spite of all the snow. The bergschrund could be easily crossed, exactly in line with the avalanche furrow.

We returned to the hut, not very pleased with the results of our examination. We felt, to put it mildly, as though our minds were weighed down by the whole mass of ice overhanging the slope. We were both of much the same opinion and took particular pleasure in enumerating the delights of this exceptional type of climb—avalanches, wet, cold, etc.

It was in very pessimistic mood that we arrived back at the Col du Géant, in thick mist, but luckily Bareux's cooking and a cheerful party of tourists soon restored our good humour. A brunette with an incredible Tyrolean hat wanted to know about our doings:

"What do you do up there always by yourselves?"

"Nothing, at the moment."

"But don't you climb?"

"No, we don't even climb."

"Well, you must get bored stiff!"

It would certainly have been more agreeable to have gone

picking bilberries in the woods of Courmayeur with such a charming girl. But then, we were a bit mad, anyone could see that. And she must have thought so, too, for she made it quite plain how much she pitied us before she left the hut.

As usual, we lay down on our bunks in the afternoon. Optimism had returned; of course the couloir would go all right, in fact it was just made to be climbed. Otherwise why was it there, in full view, for everyone to see?

So it came about that we suddenly convinced ourselves the climb was ripe for plucking, and we fixed the time to wake and set off. Then Chabod received a wire which upset everything. He had to return to Turin immediately and I went down to Courmayeur with him.

Two days later we were back at the hut again. The weather was still unsettled: from time to time a patch of blue broke the uniform grey of the skies. On August 12 we once again put on our skis and ran down in mist on the glacier below the Col du Géant. We followed the track leading to the Col du Midi for a while, then struck straight up towards the bergschrund of the couloir with the intention of crossing it and cutting steps part of the way up the slope in order to make things easier the following morning when it would be dark.

At the foot of the avalanche cone we stopped.

"Look," said Chabod, pointing to the characteristic deeply-furrowed groove to be found in all couloirs, "we shall do well to follow the groove to begin with; it'll feel less exposed there, and that's where the angle is least steep. Of course there is one drawback . . . the avalanches . . . but they come so seldom!"

And to give added weight to his theory, he began to tell me the story of a well-known French guide who . . . He was interrupted by a terrific rumble which made us look up. Out of the mist which lay motionless upon the summits above there surged a great white cloud; in a few seconds it came rushing down the couloir and spread out with a hiss over the slope. Some blocks of ice hurtled down almost as far as where we stood. There was no more talk of the groove! We agreed at once that the best way up the slope was over on the left where it was steepest, but at least slightly sheltered. All the same, we still had to start up the groove. I suggested going up and cutting steps on the first part. Chabod had no liking for it and maintained that we should be able to go up just as rapidly on our twelve-pointed Grivel crampons. However I wouldn't give way, and I crossed the bergschrund and got into the groove. I hadn't gone three yards when a flurry of powdery snow shot down and sprinkled me from head to foot. Startled, I looked up, while the small stream of snow grew larger, became a torrent and covered me completely. Was it the forerunner of another avalanche? I hurried to get down and slid beneath the upper lip of the bergschrund. Chabod was there too, and he looked at me ironically, while I swore.

"Having another go?"

"To hell with you!" I shot down the slope with Chabod at my heels. In twenty minutes we were back at our skis, and by midday at the hut. We spent the afternoon lying on our bunks and, in order to husband our nervous energy, forced ourselves not to think of the couloir. We turned in after an early supper.

At 2.20 a.m. we left the hut. Early morning starts by lantern-light seem to resemble each other, but in fact each of them evokes its own associations, its particular sensations, born in the silence of the midnight walk. We passed the Col des Flambeaux, ran down the glacier in the deep tracks leading to the Col du Midi, came to the bergschrund, and put on our crampons. It was zero hour.

At 4.30 Chabod crossed the bergschrund. As usual there was a ceaseless flow of fresh snow coming down the groove. He climbed up in the bed of the furrow for forty feet and then went out on to the slope on the left. When it came to my turn, I went as fast as I could, but was still not able to avoid being sprinkled with snow like a miller. I joined Chabod on the edge of the groove, and then he went on for another rope-length. When we were together again he tested the snow with his axe; it was deep and not consolidated.

"If it's like this everywhere we shall be in a nice fix."

"Let's hope it won't be."

We glanced below. We were only a few yards from the

bergschrund, and in ten minutes we could have been down again; and below the bergschrund lay those inviting easy slopes. Then we looked up: the wall of white above us climbed almost vertically to merge with the sky and was touched here and there to blue in the light of dawn. How many hours should we be on it?

"What about it?"

"Well, shall we?"

"Yes, let's."

The decision once taken, we went straight ahead. I took the first lead and then we changed over at the end of each run-out. Progress is much faster and less tiring this way, and one is belayed the whole time. A little higher up the snow improved and held perfectly. For two and a half hours we climbed steadily, using only the front points of our twelve-pointed Grivel crampons, and gained about a thousand feet in height. In the anxiety of the ascent we had forgotten all about the sun, which was then high above the Périades and shining full on us. But it had not forgotten its usual daily task and beneath our feet, which had to be placed with meticulous care, the snow gave way, reminding us of hard reality. The situation might well become awkward and we stopped a while to consider. The entire slope was softening up under its thick covering of snow.

We examined the rocks on the left—they were very steep and covered with verglas and we could not even have got on to them. Meanwhile there was a change in the sky. The little fish-shaped cloud which at dawn had capped the Aiguille Verte, had grown bigger and was gradually covering all the Aiguilles. This might well be our chance: for the first time in our climbing careers we prayed for bad weather. If the sky should cloud over the temperature would drop and the snow would consolidate. Otherwise we should have to stop where we were, hollow out a hole in the snow and wait until the late afternoon when the sun had circled round and everything had frozen up again. And that would obviously mean a bivouac beneath the wall of séracs.

The prospect of a forced halt of twenty hours, stuck on an ice

shoot nearly 3,000 feet high, was anything but attractive. So
we decided to climb up a bit further while waiting to see how
things developed. It was my turn to lead and I began going up
and traversing to the right because the rocks above us curved
over and jutted out into the couloir. I cleared away the soft
snow until I came to solid ice and put in a piton for a belay.
Then I continued slowly, and before cutting each step in
the ice I had the laborious and dangerous task of clearing
away the snow. An hour went by during which we advanced
only two rope-lengths. The storm which had been threatening
was now in full blast; the sun had disappeared behind a curtain
of swirling snowflakes and the snow had begun to harden.
After the traverse Chabod took over. We were able to crampon
again and went straight up towards the centre of the couloir.

The slope here steepened progressively—particularly by
comparison with the furrow which was now on our right—
because the true right bank of the couloir, up which our route
lay, ended in a side slope up against very steep rocks. A short
traverse to the right, in powder snow, gave Chabod work
similar to that on the previous traverse, but happily it did not
last long. After this we were able to continue without incident
as far as the great funnel beneath the ice wall. Forty yards
to our left a hump-backed snow rib ran up very steeply and
petered out beneath the séracs. It was this pitch that brought
us to the crux of the climb—it was also the steepest and most
exposed part of the whole ascent.

To reach it we had to traverse over bare ice, polished by
avalanches coming down from the séracs. It happened to be
my turn to lead off at the start of the traverse. Chabod saw
by my face that I was about to protest and he hastened to
assure me that in such a position it would definitely not be
advisable to change the order of the party. I swore beneath
my breath that the exit through the séracs would certainly not
find me in the lead, and after putting in a piton and arranging
a running belay, I began to cut steps. After the traverse we
cramponed up the rib—a very steep pitch indeed. Of the man
in front one saw only the bottom of his rucksack and the eight
points of his crampons that were not in contact with the snow

which, happily, was hard and in excellent condition. In our opinion the angle of the slope approached 60° and this was borne out by subsequent calculations made from measurements taken by Charles Vallot.

At the top of the rib we came up against the vertical wall of the sérac, whose edge, a few yards over to the left, limited our view. Beyond this point our fate would be decided. Suppose it was impossible to get through—the very thought of having to go down all we had come up made me catch my breath. We were like two prisoners awaiting sentence. But before we gave up, we would put all we knew into forcing a way. With infinite precaution Chabod began the traverse. I watched him climb up a little, then he moved round and disappeared from view.

"What can you see?"

"Nothing."

"Well, then we're still where we were."

"Come along."

I joined him, and he went on again and once more disappeared.

"Can you see anything now?" I asked, in a voice trembling with impatience.

"Mist . . ."

"Better and better!"

The frozen rope ran out through my hands. There came a sudden cry:

"We're through!"

Then it was my turn and soon I was beside him. We had rounded the sérac and through swirling mist we caught glimpses of a snow slope ahead leading to the ridge; it was extremely steep for the first fifty yards and then eased off. We climbed up a few rope-lengths, with our hearts in our mouths, then came out on to the ridge, into the open. Here we were exposed to the full fury of the gale; while we were in the couloir we had been sheltered from the wind, which was blowing from the south-west. Bent double, we pushed on, and in ten minutes reached the east summit. It was 1.30. We had taken exactly 8 hours 40 minutes; a relatively short time for a great climb, but it had seemed endless. In climbs of this order there is not a moment's respite from the nervous tension, and no means of resting in any peace or comfort.

We sheltered as best we could behind a boulder to eat something; Chabod's feet were hurting and he took off his crampons. It was too cold to stop long, and in a quarter of an hour we were on our feet again and beginning the descent. When I came to the west summit I did not notice that I had overshot the mark and that instead of following the right route I had embarked on the slope running down towards the Col Maudit. Shouts from Chabod at last succeeded in making me retrace my steps, and after a brief détour we got back on to the route and made our way down blindly, crouching beneath the snow squalls, with the wind whipping particles of ice into our faces. At a sudden break in the clouds we realised that we were again off the route; we were too low and too far to the right. We climbed up a bit and started in the right direction once more, continuing in a straight line over wind-beaten crusted snow, straining our eyes in the diffused, featureless light, where everything was blurred, in an effort to pick out any change in the slope.

There was a sudden sharp crack and a slow rustling in the mist. For a moment I felt almost giddy, uncertain whether I was moving or standing still, and everything seemed to spin round me. Was it a trick of the imagination? A shout from Chabod brought me back to reality:

"What's happened?"

I found myself at a standstill, one knee flexed, my axe thrust deep in the snow. Both to the right and to the left there was a clean break about a foot high, disappearing into the mist. Silently and treacherously, the avalanche had started beneath my feet, and gone hissing down the slope, to pile up on the level below. We could see nothing, and were in no position to estimate its size. We stayed there for a moment, nonplussed. Deprived of support from below, the slope above now hung over us alarmingly: if it should break away, we should be lost. Along the smooth line of cleavage, a few cracks were visible. I went down fifteen feet, then I stopped, found a providential small crevasse into which I thrust a leg and settled myself

firmly. Chabod now began to descend. Gently! But it was no
use: beneath his weight a large lozenge-shaped slab, cracked
by the pressure of the avalanche, broke away and crashed down
on to me. I bent over, braced myself with all my strength and
took the shock on my shoulder. The block split in two and all
was well! We joined up on the firm snow and ran down
without a word. When we were just above the bergschrund,
the mist lifted a minute and allowed us to take a quick look
round. We stood aghast. The whole snow slope over a distance of two hundred yards had broken away and had slid
right down to the plateau where it had piled up in a jumble of
blocks.

Once again we looked at the upper part of the slope which, so
very fortunately for us, had remained hanging up there, then
we turned and went down towards the bergschrund. We
found a way across on the right by the rocks, and in a quarter
of an hour we came to the Aiguille du Midi tracks. At 5.45 we
were back at the Torino.

During a brief conversation at the Torino hut Lucien Devies
had promised me he would return to Entrèves. He arrived by
car from Grindelwald, where he had been with Lagarde, and
came to find me at the *Casa dell' Alpinista* where I had been
taking it easy for a few days. I was deep in an enthralling game
of chess when he asked me point-blank if I would care to
go with him to the Dauphiné in pursuit of a still virgin north
face.

Frankly, when I heard of a 3,000-foot wall, it set my pulse
racing! So far no rock climbs of extreme difficulty (the *Très
Difficile* or *T. D.* category) had been made on the French side
of the Alps: this might be the first. My interest was enhanced
by a wish to compensate for our latest defeat on the Jorasses,
and also by the great attraction of these mountains which were
quite new to me, but which I had often admired from the
peaks round Susa. So I accepted with enthusiasm.

The Dauphiné was then almost totally unexplored by
climbers using modern techniques. The greatest climbs to date
were those of the Mayer-Dibona party on the south wall of the

Meije, and the Costa Rouge ridge of the Ailefroide, but among
the wild peaks of the Dauphiné were still to be found several
of the hardest problems remaining in the Alps.

We left Courmayeur on August 19. Each of us felt we had
found a real friend, we shared so many interests and ideas.
Our new alliance would be tested and proved by many a hard
trial to come. While the car tore up the slopes of the Petit St
Bernard we completed the mental preparation for our climb—
not the least of the pleasures of mountaineering. Devies knew
of the north-west face of the Olan only from photographs—so
that one could fill in his picture freely from one's imagination.
We reached Grenoble the same day and stopped there to collect information and call upon some friends of Devies. On the
21st we continued to le Désert-en-Val-Jouffrey where we left
the car, and after lunch set out, burdened with enormous
rucksacks crammed with all our equipment and food for
several days. To add to our discomfort a thick layer of cloud
spread across the sky, which boded anything but good weather
for climbing. Plodding up a steep path, in a damp rainy atmosphere with a back-breaking load on one's shoulders, is always
fatal to morale.

Then at a turn of the valley, the Olan appeared. The summit was shrouded in mist, but this made the wall stand out all
the more powerfully in the deep shadow of its cloud cap. The
vision of our peak lying before us wrapped in still virgin
mystery, at the end of a remote and almost entirely unfrequented valley, quickly restored our enthusiasm.

At the hut there would be no guardian, no climbers in this
cul-de-sac, and no prying telescopes would follow our steps to
give us, perhaps, some slight hope of rescue in case of need.
Up there we should be as alone as if we were a thousand miles
from civilisation. Forward, then! We pressed on eagerly in
the rain.

Early in the morning of August 22 we left on a reconnaissance, going up to the foot of the great central couloir, but we
were unable to ascertain much except the frequency of falling
stones. We came down and crossed towards the slopes opposite
the wall. In spite of the pall of mist which hid the mountains,

we were able to see enough to make a cursory examination. The wall springs from the little Olan glacier, and rises in a Dolomitic sweep of over 3,500 feet. It is split down the centre, from summit to base, by an immense couloir which slants across at the top towards the second summit, a hundred feet or so lower than the main peak.

Two obvious routes immediately strike the eye: the first, to the left of the couloir, runs straight up to the main summit; the second would entail following the edge of the couloir on the right, then climbing up in it to within three hundred feet of the ridge, and finally traversing across and coming out on the summit of the subsidiary peak. The first was the ideal line, but on examining it through the glasses we saw that the final 1,600 feet would only be possible with the aid of pitons [1] and, remaining faithful to our tradition of tackling only those climbs which we could do without artificial aids, we discarded it. The second route, however, looked climbable throughout —except for a steep portion of yellow rock—and we settled on it. Having made this decision, we returned to the hut.

Contrary to expectations the weather seemed on the mend. In the evening the moon shone through drifting cloud, flooding the valley with light and shadow, and under the stars the mountains looked eternally new, eternally beautiful.

When we left the hut at 4 a.m. on the 23rd, the moon had disappeared behind the mountains and we had to light the lantern. At 5.15 we stopped at the upper edge of the glacier, beneath a protecting overhang, twenty yards to the right of the black dripping wall at the bottom of the couloir. It was cold and in the perfectly clear sky a few wisps of mist floated, carried on the still south-west wind, and touched with red by the sun.

Walking up rather quickly had made us sweat and during our brief halt the moisture seemed to freeze beneath our clothes. We hurriedly changed our boots for espadrilles and roped up on our two hundred-foot ropes. At 5.50 I started up the rocks; the first step consisted of a long stride. Right from the beginning, the difficulties were uniform and sustained. We

[1] This direct route was climbed in August 1956 by Jean Couzy and René Desmaisons with three bivouacs and 89 pitons. [*Translators' Note.*]

were anxious to get to the most difficult pitches and we climbed quickly; after two and a half hours' uneasy climbing, almost always following a straight line, with only occasional deviations to either side, we came to the top of the initial spur and reached a shoulder where the angle eased off a little. We had climbed some 1,300 feet and had come to the edge where the couloir fans out into a bowl. Ahead of us the wall steepened again. On the left, beneath the summit, was the great step, which we hoped to attempt at some future date. Clouds began to appear in the sky, but we hoped the fine weather would last out at least till evening. After building a cairn we continued obliquely to the right over broken rock towards a big vertical black chimney, but without going right up to it. The wall steepened and the difficulties increased. Here, for six or seven hundred feet, there was an uninterrupted series of very difficult and beautiful pitches: on this sheer wall the exposure was tremendous. At the end of each run-out we belayed to a piton.

Then the difficulties decreased, but this merely enabled us to get a better view of the great menacing wall above—the yellow rock we had spotted from below, which constituted the crux of the climb. A few more rope-lengths brought us to the foot. It was split by a crack that soared skywards, but to reach it one had first to climb a smooth, almost holdless slab.

I lost no time in attacking the slab on the left, but after ten feet I could get no further up nor was I able to traverse across. Then Lucien, who was below and to the right, suggested I should try on that side, so I came down and made an attempt there, climbing up slowly and with difficulty. Going over to the left I succeeded, by making a long stride, in getting to the crack, but loose blocks made the start impossible. I was in a most precarious position and after desperate efforts I succeeded in knocking in a piton and clipping my rope on to it with a karabiner.

"Pull in!" Supported slightly by the piton, which did not seem very secure, I managed to push the threatening blocks off into space.

"Slack off gently!" I recovered my balance and then forced my way up into the crack. I was beginning to feel I had had enough. I came to a niche, put in a piton, and brought up the rucksacks, but as there was not room for the two of us I went on a few more yards and then told Lucien to come up. As soon as he joined me, I went on again, for my anxiety to see how we were going to get up outweighed my longing for a rest.

At 2.30 we came out on to the crest of the rib forming the true left bank of the couloir, and here we stopped to rest and eat. Victory now seemed assured—too easy, even. Ahead of us there was still a succession of vertical pitches, difficult but fairly short. Higher up the angle decreased and the wall led up to the right of the upper part of the great couloir, as seen from below.

At 3.15 we started again, intending to go on until the main difficulties were passed and then traverse across the couloir and climb straight up to the summit of the central or secondary peak. But once more we had counted our chickens too soon. Since a bivouac on the summit was now a certainty, we were almost sorry not to find any more difficulties to tackle and overcome; but then, suddenly, we were caught up in an eddy of mist. In a few minutes it had thickened and spread, blinding us and destroying all sense of direction.

We still went on, feeling our way up smooth and sometimes verglas-coated rocks. At 5 o'clock the hail started, but a distant roll of thunder showed that the storm was not yet upon us. On our right we found a ledge, and with the hail now falling thicker, there was nothing for it but to stop. Without undue difficulty we arranged our Zdarsky tent and, about 6 o'clock, just as the hail changed to wet snow, we crept inside.

The exalted state of mind in which we had begun the climb, —a state now reinforced by the fact that we had already glimpsed victory close at hand—enabled us to contemplate this setback, hazardous as it well might be, with quiet confidence. I would almost say with joy, were it not for my fear of being taken severely to task by some stern critic of the risks of mountaineering. To pass the time and help forget the cold while we waited to see what the weather might do, we told each other about our mountain adventures and made plans for future expeditions together. As we talked we discovered a perfect identity of outlook which would bring us closer, strengthen our new friendship, and enable us to form a strong and united partnership in our future undertakings.

Meanwhile the storm broke over us in an awe-inspiring crescendo. It raged that night over the whole of the Western Alps and stranded a number of climbers in the Mont Blanc district, with grave consequences, as we learned later, to a French party who were involved in a tragic adventure on the Peuterey ridge.

Hail squalls beat against the Zdarsky which we were at pains to keep close up against the rock in order to conserve the slight warmth generated by our bodies. The lightning was continuous and the electricity with which the atmosphere was overcharged struck the mountain over and over again. The rock seemed to vibrate and tremble ceaselessly, as though it was a living thing. From time to time thunder awoke the echoes in every couloir, battering down our confidence and making us realise how for all our exhilaration we might at any moment be hurled into space.

Once the full violence of the storm had passed the snow began to fall; and, with all the hazards it would bring with it the next day, snow was the most serious thing for us. Our exaltation vanished and we began to envisage the possible consequences of our situation. Our few remaining provisions would certainly not enable us to hold out for more than a day; therefore (putting aside the possible solution—if conditions improved—of roping down the 3,000-foot wall) there was nothing for it but to force a way upwards whatever the weather and whatever the conditions. But should we succeed in overcoming the cold and the snow? This question tormented us for the rest of the night, and so did the cold which became more penetrating with every passing hour.

At 3 o'clock in the morning the snow stopped. The wind began to tear at the clouds and through the rifts we saw moonlight. Hope was renewed and helped us through the last three hours of waiting. At 6 o'clock we threw off the tent and stood up in the cutting wind. It took us nearly half an hour to pack up our sacks and untangle the ropes. The sky was still stormy, and heavy mists lay motionless in the hollow of the valley.

The rocks were covered with a thick layer of frozen snow. We should have to hurry, and by 6.30 we were off. After a few yards our light espadrilles were soaked and our feet icy; I tried climbing with my gloves on, but very soon I had to take them off and then hands and feet were in the same condition. The day before we had complained that the difficulties were over too soon. Now they reappeared, and formidable they were. It was no longer a question of forcing a way up difficult rocks, but of the still greater difficulties caused by the unforeseen complications of snow and ice, wind and cold. In this fight to the death we were no longer climbing to conquer; we had to conquer to survive.

Our finger-tips were already worn by long hours of rock-climbing, and the cold and wet wore the skin still further, leaving the flesh raw. Happily, cold numbs all feeling, and if it makes it harder to grip the rock, it does at least deaden the pain.

Nevertheless we progressed, gaining ground yard by yard. On this part of the climb, where under normal conditions one would go full speed ahead, there are no real pitches. I remember only manœuvres with a rope reduced to a tangle of knots, frequent belaying on rickety pitons, and a traverse where it was touch and go whether the snow would hold or not.

After nearly five hours, we at last reached the ridge. This time our determination had finally triumphed over circumstances. We had managed to reach our goal in the brief space of four days, notwithstanding uncertain weather conditions and in spite of our being on totally unknown ground.

Content with this rather arrogant view of things we allowed ourselves a long halt, cheered by the sun when it occasionally succeeded in piercing the clouds. Slightly before 1 o'clock, with the mists once more shrouding the mountain, we began the descent of the west ridge which is easy, but long and jagged; towards evening we entered the hut with but one thought: to stop and lie down, no matter where, provided there was a roof overhead.

Next morning I went up the short length of glacier in espadrilles to get to the foot of the climb and retrieve our boots and ice-axes; then in the afternoon we went down to Fond-Turbat and on to Grenoble by car. Lucien returned to Paris and I went back to Italy via Modane. Before saying goodbye to the mountains for the season I still hoped to spend ten days in the Dolomites.

At Turin I found a letter from Pasquale Palazzo, whose acquaintance I had made at Naples in the spring; he wrote saying that he had spent the summer in the Dolomites and felt in good training for a big climb. I made a rendezvous with him at the Vazzoler hut for the middle of September.

We repeated the Videsott route on the Busazza and then decided to attempt the spigolo of the Torre Trieste.

The Torre Trieste, a pillar which conforms to the classic structure of a Dolomite peak, adjoins the gigantic citadel of the northern Civetta group. It is separated from the Busazza by a gap high up, so that it stands out only when seen from the Vazzoler hut, or better still from the path going up to it from Cencenighe. There are few precipices of more forbidding aspect than this face. This year Carlesso and Sandri had succeeded, after a climb of extreme severity, in conquering the south face, but the most elegant problem—that of the south-east spigolo—was still unsolved, and would undoubtedly be one of the finest climbs in the Dolomites.

We set out for it two days after climbing the Busazza, without really meaning to make a full-scale attempt, but with the idea of making a prolonged reconnaissance, and finding out the difficulties of the first section, which coincided with Carlesso's route. After climbing a plinth of rocks covered with dwarf pines, we continued up for three rope-lengths of considerable difficulty; then, on the first pitch where pitons had been used, we had a nasty set-back. Carlesso had a habit of driving pitons into cracks where they would penetrate barely an inch. I had already found this out at the first piton we came to, but I reckoned that if they had held the others they would hold me too. So, hoping for the best, I left my narrow ledge and was in process of climbing up the wall above it, using the pitons already in position, when the top one suddenly shot out of the rock. The jerk pulled three other pitons out, one after the other; only the last one held. There I was dangling in space, with a rope hitched under one leg holding me upside-down, so that I was able to contemplate at leisure the splendid panorama spread out beneath me. Cautiously Palazzo let me down a few yards as far as the ledge where I arrived in a sitting position. Then, in order to free the rope round my leg, I caught hold of it beneath me and started to untwist it. This eased the continued tension on the piton that had held me so magnificently and, no doubt assuming that it had now completed its mission, it proceeded to drop down like a ripe pear! I was much moved by this kindly attention and I still have the piton which I keep as a precious talisman.

Thinking of what might have happened, we both agreed that the reconnaissance had been highly successful; and in three rappels we were down at the bottom. But in my fall I had twisted my foot, and the pain was aggravated by the descent. So, abandoning our brilliant project, we both returned home.

Six : 1935

IN the spring of 1935 there was a feeling in the air that the hour had struck for the Grandes Jorasses. It was essential to be ready for action early in the season, so Chabod and I decided to go up to the Leschaux hut on June 30, though we were pretty sure that this date would be a bit premature. But that year weather conditions followed a cycle which convinced us that one should not always rely on accepted ideas. Up to mid-June snow fell without a break, then it stopped and without any warning there began a series of exceptionally hot days. This did not melt the thick snow off sloping walls and faces, but it did make a clean sweep of every steep wall and, because June is the month when the sun is highest in the sky, even of those that faced north.

But we were not able to foresee all this in time. So, after staying four days in the Grignetta—a limestone massif near Lecco—we left for the Val d'Aosta, thinking there was no need to hurry, for we could see the snow was still lying thick on the mountains all round. So we decided to complete our training by making an attempt on the still virgin wall of Mont Emilius above the Val d'Aosta—there was a virtual taboo on it because of the tragic outcome of the attempt made by the Charrey brothers. Chabod had his own personal reasons for wanting to do this climb, and I had a particular interest in it too, because of a bet that I had made with Andrea Brezzi during a short visit to Cogne. On June 26 we went up to the hunting-lodge belonging to the Peccoz family, who had most obligingly given us the run of the place, and had sent one of their game-wardens along with us. On the 27th we attacked the face, equipped for a prolonged struggle and for a bivouac. Actually a surprise was in store, for we found that, although the difficulties were sustained and uniform, they never exceeded a low grade IV standard. We climbed the 1,300 feet to the summit in four and a half hours and were able to return the same evening to Quart where we spent the night.

On the 28th we were in Courmayeur. It was still very hot, and the run of fine weather continued. We crossed the Col du Géant, taking the winter route by the Toule glacier, for there was still a great deal of snow on the rock spur where the normal summer path zigzags up. After spending the night at the Torino, on June 30 we went down to the Leschaux hut. At about 10 in the morning, when we reached the point on the glacier from which you can see the north face of the Grandes Jorasses, we could scarcely believe our eyes. The wall was in wonderful condition, dry and bare as we never remembered seeing it before.

"I bet the whole crowd are on the face today," said Chabod, "Germans, French, Swiss, and I shouldn't be surprised if there were some Japs as well!"

He was only too right. As soon as we reached the hut, we saw a climber with a funereal expression on his face, gazing upwards. It was the German Steinauer, the climbing companion of Franz Schmid, the conqueror of the north face of the Matterhorn, and he also had arrived late on the scene. He greeted us by name, then with outstretched arm he pointed to the wall: "*Peters in der Wand.*"

"Since when?" we asked. But he did not know. The guardian came out and told us that the two Germans, Martin Meier and Rudolf Peters, had gone past three days ago without even stopping at the hut. Since then nobody had heard of them. The Swiss climbers Roch and Gréloz had also attacked the face that morning, as well as two Frenchmen, Edouard Frendo and Chaix, from the Ecole de Haute Montagne.

So our hopes of three years were dashed to the ground. Chabod's reaction was to say that he didn't want to have anything more to do with this face, and that the only thing was to pack our sacks and be off. But the news had made me furious; and I declared that now we were at the Leschaux we would get on to the wall, come what might. And anyway it was by no means impossible that we should find the Germans held up somewhere. After his outburst Chabod also came round to the view that we must make an attempt, and we decided to start at 1 o'clock next morning.

At midday we were surprised to see four men descending the glacier—the Swiss and French parties. Gréloz had dislocated his shoulder and they had had to turn back. So there was nobody but the Germans ahead of us, and if they were not dead by now they must surely have succeeded. In the afternoon the guide Lambert and Mademoiselle Boulaz, who had already made an attempt the year before, arrived at the hut. When they learned of our intention to start out for the face, they came to tell us that they would be doing the same. Then we all went to bed.

First up and first to leave the hut were Lambert and Loulou Boulaz, but they stopped at the foot of the wall beneath the bergschrund, and waited for us; it was clear that they had hurried with this end in view. At 3.45 Renato crossed the bergschrund and began the work of cutting steps up the initial slope, which was bare ice. We gained height rapidly on these pitches, which were already familiar to us, and Chabod suggested a slight variation which made this first section easier. At 7.30 we came to the second tower, and at 8 o'clock we were back on the crest of the spur. Meanwhile the sun had begun to touch the upper slopes, loosing the first furious volley of stones as an ominous greeting from the wall above.

By 8.45 we had reached the beginning of the lower névé where we had stopped the year before. This lower part of the climb was made very much easier this year by the quite exceptional conditions of the mountain. We traversed slowly across the ice-slope to the right, taking it in turns to cut steps so as to husband our strength.

At 10.30 we were at the foot of the famous band of slabs which constitutes the crux of the face. A concealed slanting dièdre—or open groove—appeared to be the most vulnerable point. We thought the Germans had taken this way, and in fact, as soon as I started up the groove I found pitons at the back of it. The pitch was polished by water trickling down and looked extremely hard. I put on espadrilles and began to climb. When I came to the second piton, I could see quite clearly that it was very much easier on the right, where from the beginning Renato had wanted me to try. I traversed across, using the rope until I was clear of the groove, and here I found excellent holds which enabled me to climb straight up without using pitons. Then I came back to the left above the groove, thus by-passing the artificial pitch. A crack brought me out on to a ledge like the lid of a desk, where Peters and Haringer had probably bivouacked the year before. After this pitch the difficulties increased and so did the danger of falling stones. Below the barrier of slabs the steepness of the wall had protected us a little, whereas above it the stones ricocheted all over the place and some fell close beside us.

While we were busy with the crux of the climb, great clouds began to form on the summits, thunder rumbled in the distance, and one of those violent, shattering storms you get in the high mountains suddenly broke over us. At the same moment the Swiss couple appeared on the platform, and finding themselves precariously placed they asked anxiously for a rope, which Chabod hurried to give them. So there we were, all four anchored to pitons, and there we remained for perhaps an hour while the hail beat down on us.

This storm was one of the most awe-inspiring spectacles I have ever seen in the high Alps. The upper part of the face acted as a gathering ground for all the hail that did not lodge on the rocks. Small avalanches formed, got up speed on the upper névé and then came pouring down on the slabs where we had stopped. With incredible violence the torrent struck us squarely, and if the pitons had not been well and truly driven in we should have been swept away like straws.

After the fury of the hurricane had abated the wall was a fearful sight. But now we were in full cry. We had already climbed more than half the face, and with the knowledge that others had gone before us we were determined not to give up. So the decision to continue was made and we remained roped together as a party of four. In the position in which the storm had stopped us—that is to say right in the middle of a pitch—it was impossible for me to change back into my boots, which anyway were in Chabod's sack, fifty feet below. So I was obliged to continue in espadrilles. Slowly, I started climbing again, clearing the hail from the holds, blowing on my hands to warm them and belaying myself frequently with pitons. I continued in this way for two rope-lengths, then I traversed over to the left towards the upper névé, where I was able to put on my boots.

We halted here in a sort of niche hollowed out in the ice beneath a big boulder. It was the most roomy spot that we found on the whole face, and gave us shelter from the blast of an absolutely icy wind which now swept the face and froze our sodden clothes. We were completely enveloped in mist. Though the fury of the storm had abated, bad weather had set in, and huge clouds rolled along in a wild sky.

The main difficulties should, by rights, have been behind us, but we did not know whether we should be able to finish the climb in the conditions in which we now found it. Nevertheless, we decided without further ado to go on and bivouac as high up as possible. To speed matters up, we reverted to two ropes of two, put on our crampons, and Chabod began to cut steps on the upper névé. At first the two Swiss had wanted to bivouac where they were, but Renato yelled down a warning—and quite rightly too—that if they remained there they ran the risk of being caught like rats in a trap. This stirred them to action and they followed us up the ice-slope.

At the top of the névé I took over the lead again; we were once more on broken rock, which would have been easy if dry, but had become extremely dangerous in present conditions. Loose holds were cemented by ice and it was impossible to distinguish them from genuinely good ones. A few rope-lengths brought us to the foot of a chimney which ran up to a gap on the spur. We tried to bear over to the right to gain the great

gully which lies to the right of the Pointe Croz, for we thought
this was the way the Germans had taken. But in making an
attempt to get round, I let slip a piton just as I was driving it
in, and it flew out into space. In trying to save this valuable
object, I made a sudden move which jerked the block on which
I was standing; it gave way under the strain and I went with it.
Fortunately the piton I had put in for a belay thirty feet lower
down, and to which the rope was clipped, held firm and
Chabod was easily able to take the strain.

"Are you hurt?" he cried anxiously.

"No. My hands are a bit grazed, that's all, and I've knocked
my back, but it's nothing much."

I traversed to the left and stopped on a ledge where Chabod
joined me. As it was getting dark we decided to go up the
chimney, where we ought to be able to find somewhere to
bivouac. Renato wished to take the lead so that I could rest a
bit, but I refused and went on, for I wanted to counteract the
shock of the fall.

At 9 o'clock we stopped to bivouac, but it could hardly
have been called a convenient spot. The two Swiss were able
to settle themselves in more comfortably than we could, sitting
on an overhanging ledge with their feet dangling in the air.
But we had to stay on our feet, anchored to pitons, unable
even to get inside the bivouac sack—one of us on a projecting
spike of rock at the back of the chimney, the other hanging
straddled across. Every half hour we changed places. Very
soon the bitter cold began to penetrate and our clothes turned
to suits of icy armour. From the overhang above a little stream
trickled down, which we were in no position to dodge, and
from time to time an avalanche of stones went humming past
in the dark. Eight hours went by like this.

We were on the move next morning at 5 o'clock. We climbed
up to the gap; then, high up, we bore considerably to the right,
traversing across a short ice-slope. But as soon as I had rounded
the central rib which drops straight down from the Pointe Croz
a fearsome sight came into view: the gully by which we hoped
to reach safety was one immense unbroken sheet of ice with a
few polished rocks sticking out here and there. Yesterday's hail,

which had melted and then frozen during the night, was responsible for this pretty piece of work.

I brought Chabod up beside me so that we could make a joint decision; and we agreed that it was impossible to finish the climb that way.

"There are no two ways about it," muttered Renato, "we are properly beaten, and on our own ground. I suggest we try the rib on the left."

We retraced our steps and called to Lambert, who was awaiting our decision on the other side of the rib, to begin climbing up so as not to waste time. And just then, as if to underline the dramatic character of the moment, the hail started. But it stopped again in a minute. If we could not force a way up the rib we were lost. Five hundred feet—perhaps only four hundred —separated us from the summit; yet there we were, caught in an icy trap. But the moment of despair had passed and as we traversed back across the ice-slope we gripped our axes as though we would crush them to splinters. Up we would go at all costs, for our lives depended on it.

"Is this the way?" the Swiss asked when we joined them.

"Maybe," we answered briefly, for we did not want to scare them since they had blindly entrusted themselves to our leadership. We climbed up the rib over sound rock and glazed slabs to within a hundred feet of the summit, where further progress seemed to be barred by an overhang. It would be a joke in the worst of taste if we were not able to force this last pitch. I took off my sack, hooking it to a piton, and went to the attack. The rock was very friable and the pitons did not hold. I made my way up very slowly with extreme caution, for my fingers were damaged by frost-bite and hurt like hell. Eventually I succeeded in wedging myself into the final crack, fifteen feet beneath the exit, and there I was able to put in a piton and rest on it for a bit before going on again. The top was easier, and a last effort brought me out on the summit. We had won, and we were saved.

I settled myself on the ridge, hauled up the sacks and brought Chabod up. Then I dropped the rope down to Lambert whose frozen fingers were so swollen that he could not grip the rock. After a few more efforts we were all assembled together on the top—in thick mist, but this no longer worried us.

We climbed up to the Pointe Whymper and then began the descent. On the easy slabs of the Rochers Whymper I started a stately glissade which, had not Chabod braced himself and held firm, would have ended in my sailing down the full length of the ordinary route on the Grandes Jorasses—a most un-dignified ending to the climb up the north face![1]

Once off the rocks, instead of making for the Reposoir we went straight on down the couloir. There was still a con-siderable quantity of snow and most of the crevasses below were entirely covered, so that we were able to get down with-out hindrance to the hut, which we reached at 7 o'clock. After sleeping like logs, we went down next morning to Courmayeur and from there to Turin.

A week later we again made our way over the Col du Géant and down to the Leschaux hut to pick up our big rucksacks. Then we went on to stay at the Montenvers with the intention of making an attempt on the north face of the Drus. But once again the weather was uncertain; so were our plans, on account of Renato's feet, which had suffered on the Jorasses bivouac because of old frostbite, and were still giving trouble. One morning I went off alone to make a reconnaissance as far as the foot of the north face of the Drus. When I returned I found Renato's feet were no better and he told me that, very natur-ally, a second bivouac made no appeal to him. So we gave up the Drus and made our way back to the Col du Géant.

At the Torino we found Boccalatte and Nini Pietrasanta, so we decided to join forces for an attempt on the Pic Adolphe Rey, a striking pinnacle of rock which had succeeded in re-maining inviolate in spite of all attacks. The year before Chabod and I had made two attempts on the south face while waiting for better conditions to tackle something higher, but on each occasion we had been driven back after a few rope-lengths of extreme difficulty. However in view of the exception-ally good condition of north faces this year, we again turned

[1] The German pair, Meier and Peters, had completed the first ascent forty-eight hours before.

our attention to a route which Renato had originally tried; this entailed a rappel down to the gap between the Pic Adolphe Rey and the Petit Capucin, followed by a hypothetical traverse towards a series of cracks. Gabriele, on the other hand, wished to attack the north face straight up from the foot. Finally we all agreed on the route from the gap.

From the gap we climbed up the ridge for a rope's-length to a small convenient platform where we fixed the rappel. We were climbing as one party and I went down first, followed by Chabod who would belay me for the traverse. Boccalatte came last and would not leave the platform until the key passage had been mastered, so that we could if necessary retreat. From the bottom of the rappel I climbed obliquely up the wall and after a few attempts at forcing the great vertical slabs I launched out on the traverse. At the start there was a flake which allowed me to progress elegantly in a lay-back position, but further on the crack narrowed so that I could not get my fingers in and had to summon up every subtlety of technique. I fixed some line to a piton and taking up a rappel position succeeded in moving along horizontally; with the greatest difficulty I managed to put in a piton some distance in which enabled me to go still further and then to put in another piton. In this way I reached the line of cracks. We were soon all across, and once we were assembled together, we split up into two ropes and reached the summit without any other particular difficulty, leaving in place the two key pitons which solved the problem. Our route on the descent was down the great chimney on the south face by means of long rappels, one of them a free rappel of 120 feet.

Back at the Torino we celebrated this pleasant victory joyfully, drinking the health of the "great little Adolphe", to whom, with great respect, we dedicated our climb. Unhappily it was the last climb for Renato. Through being squeezed into espadrilles, and in the cold for hours, his feet had got very much worse, and he had to give up any further activity.

It was still only July 16—what an exceptional summer it was!—and Devies was not free until early August. I went

Matterhorn from Breuil in winter

North face of Drus

Picco Gugliermina. The route lies up the pillar picked out by
the sun and shadow division

Piliers de Fresney (Frêney). The Gervasutti route takes the
wide buttress just to the left of the prominent snow couloir

down to Entrèves in rather a bad temper. The philosophical
Chabod prepared to do some painting while giving his feet
and hands a sun-cure, and I sent a wire to Gino Binaghi asking
him if he could join me in Courmayeur. I did not want to
waste this run of glorious days, so rare in the Mont Blanc
massif, and now that the Jorasses had fallen I knew that
everyone would be concentrating on the Drus.

Two days later Gino arrived, but he said he was not in
training. However, that couldn't be helped: we decided to go
up to the Torino for an attempt on the great east pillar of
Mont Blanc du Tacul and then down to the Montenvers. But
that year, as always with me, I was out of luck: indeed I had
invariably to work hard for my luck and snatch it as best I
could, forcing it to serve my own ends. On Mont Blanc du
Tacul instead of avoiding the first big gendarme, as Boccalatte
did when later he succeeded in this magnificent climb, we tried
to keep to the perfect line of ascent and we tackled the overhanging rocks where they plunged furthest down to the glacier.
After 500 feet of superb climbing we came up against an
enormous overhang which barred the way to the summit of the
gendarme.

I succeeded in getting round this practically insuperable
obstacle by forcing an extremely difficult oblique pitch. But
when my partner was half-way up this pitch he went flying,
together with the recalcitrant piton that he had been trying to
prise out. The rope did not hold him sufficiently as it was not
directly above him, and he swung out into space beneath the
overhang. The rope was still threaded through two pitons
and though I made tremendous efforts I was unable to pull
him up. The situation was becoming desperate, and all I
could do was to hold the rope tight. But fortunately Gino did
not lose his presence of mind. Although in an extremely
awkward position, he succeeded, by superhuman efforts, in
extracting some line from his sack and putting it through a piton
to which he fixed an étrier. Then, with some help from me, he
hauled himself up over the overhang and joined me.

But, after hanging on the rope for over an hour, he was
completely exhausted, and could not possibly go on. After a

long rest on the summit of the gendarme we began the descent, first by a rappel down a most beautiful vertical slab, then by the route up which we had come.

Binaghi then went off, and once again I went down to Entrèves to find someone to climb with. There were a few days of bad weather, then Colonnetti arrived from Turin, so I took the opportunity to fill in two or three days with him. We went up to the Fréboudzie bivouac-shelter meaning to climb the Petites Jorasses, take in a little unclimbed peak on the frontier ridge, and then continue to the summit. But when we were no further than the glacier, Colonnetti showed obvious signs of distress. Coming straight out from Turin with no training, he was really not up to a fairly long climb immediately, whereas I was rather keyed up by my recent adventures, and in no mood for a nice easy promenade!

We took a terribly long time to reach the col below the little peak and it looked as if we should certainly have to bivouac if we went on; so, as we were not equipped for it, I decided to go back. On the descent our pace was scarcely any faster, and on reaching the glacier we barely had time, before the last glimmer of daylight had faded, to get through the complicated network of crevasses which had to be crossed before reaching the moraine. But when the Devil takes a hand there is nothing one can do about it! While forcing the pace over the great glacial plateau, following in the tracks we had made on the ascent, I suddenly found myself confronted by an enormous crevasse, at least thirty feet wide, which had not been there in the morning. Seeing that our tracks continued on the other side it did not take me long to grasp the situation: the crevasse had been entirely covered by a vast snow bridge for a considerable distance—and we had crossed it thinking we were on solid ground! The movement of the ice had caused the bridge to collapse, and the way was now barred across the whole width of the glacier. There was nothing for it but to look for a crossing-place near the edge of the glacier close up to the rocks. We were lucky to find a fragile-looking bridge which boldly spanned the crevasse, but it wasn't an easy place to cross. To begin with there was a narrow rising crest, then a descending knife-edge ending in a vertical wall over ten feet high, down which we should have to jump. I sent Colonnetti first, thinking that over the second part I should be able to hold him better from above, but after a few yards he came down, declaring that he would prefer me to go first and hold him from the other side. This did not strike me as a very good idea, but time pressed and I agreed. I crossed the bridge as quickly as possible, jumped down on to the opposite side and, firmly belayed round my ice-axe, prepared to hold my friend. Then, with the same utter calm he had already shown in the Dolomites, up he started. But, as I had foreseen, when he reached the apex of the bridge, where it began to slope down and also to get more difficult, he flatly refused to go on. High words passed between us, which it is better not to repeat. I must have said something that reflected on his courage—and that was a most unhappy idea: for just to show that it was merely a matter of how you looked at it, Colonnetti sat down with Olympian calm upon the summit of the bridge which looked like collapsing any moment. He took his camera from his sack, and in the last glimmer of twilight proceeded impassively to take photographs. In face of such a demonstration, I lost the last trace of self-control, and declared that if he did not join me within five minutes I would unrope and go off, leaving him to his fate. He saw from my face that I was not bluffing, and he finally decided to come. But our return was now hopelessly compromised, for we had no lantern, and after wandering in the dark for another good hour, looking for the way on to the moraine, we resigned ourselves to spending the night pacing up and down the bed of a filled-in crevasse, only three-quarters of an hour from the hut.

Next day we went down to Entrèves with our tempers worn pretty thin! On the way we met some acquaintances, who gave us bad news: two of our Turin friends, Alberico and Borgna, both young men full of promise, had disappeared in the bergschrund on the Col de la Brenva, into which they had been swept by an avalanche. We hurried down to obtain more details, and when we reached the *Casa dell' Alpinista* the news was, alas, confirmed. Two more friends gone, victims of our common passion. Some people were sorry not to be able to fetch their bodies, but I felt there could be no fitter grave for the climber who falls in the mountains, than a vault of ice which enfolds and preserves him. But the public is so critical of the follies of mountaineers that I don't expect to be forgiven for holding such an opinion. Rivero and Piolti turned up at the *Casa dell' Alpinista* and we planned, and successfully carried out, a climb which we had all been very keen to do—the Hirondelles ridge of the Grandes Jorasses.

At last, at the end of July, Lucien Devies sent word that, in accordance with the programme we had already drawn up, I was to leave for Cortina, where I had also arranged to meet Amedeo Sarfatti and Pasquale Palazzo. Devies arrived from Paris, out of training except for a few visits to the Fontainebleau rocks, and all four of us went together to the spigolo of the Punta Fiammes. This climb, which ought by rights to have passed off without incident, was enlivened by some unforeseen events. To begin with, a violent rain storm, accompanied by hail, held us up half-way, but we went on as soon as the worst was over. Soon the sun shone again, and a strong wind dried both the rocks and our clothes. A rope's-length below the summit, when all the difficulties were over, I took a belay on a pillar of rock abutting on the wall, and brought up Devies; as soon as he was up, I went on. The hundred-foot rope ran out, I came to the ridge just beneath the summit and sat down, waiting for Lucien to bring up the third man to his stance. Suddenly there was an agonised cry from the invisible Devies: "Look out! Look out!" I tightened the rope round a projecting knob of rock, but I could not make out what was happening. An infernal din filled the valley, and it sounded as though the whole mountain were falling to pieces. Then it suddenly struck me—it must be the pillar! And Sarfatti and Palazzo were below. But I could not for the moment leave my place to go and see how much rock had fallen. At last Devies called to me to go down. "Is it all right?" I asked anxiously. Then Lucien explained that while he was bringing up the third member of the party, the pillar had begun to move. He had shouted to warn the others while he himself clung to the wall.

Tons of rock had fallen on to the ledge below and the two last members of the party had only just had time to take cover beneath an overhang. The rope between Lucien and the third man had been chopped into little bits, none of them more than a yard long! In the end we were none the worse except for an almighty fright, so we roped up again and finished the climb.

The following days we climbed the Guglia di Amicis and the Comici route on the Ditto Dio, then, leaving Sarfatti and Palazzo at Cortina, Lucien and I crossed the Forcella Staulanza and went up to the Coldai hut. Lucien was not in training, and after the strain of hard bivouacs and long approaches in the Western Alps I was feeling tired and slack, wanting to rest rather than make more ascents. But Lucien's holiday was limited, so we stuck to the programme we had drawn up. Although not on top of our form, we set out for the Solleder route on the Civetta. I would certainly rather have been in better shape for the ascent of this wall, as much for the sake of being able to enjoy the beauties of the climb to the full, as of having a real reserve of strength—I remembered how ill-luck had dogged my steps when climbing in this group. However, we made up for our physical shortcomings by determination, and reached the summit at 7 p.m. We stopped only a moment, then began the descent in order to avoid a bivouac, more particularly as a thick mist was rising from the valley. Suddenly we heard the sound of voices about a hundred yards below us— it was Cassin and a friend who had just done the Comici route. We joined forces and went on down together, but we couldn't see a thing in the mist and lost a lot of time, although the ordinary route is very easy. Night had fallen when we came to the one possible way down the last rock wall. As usual, we were just that half-hour too late to reach the path, and spent the night pacing up and down a ledge. From time to time it rained. When dawn broke, it took us only a few minutes to get on to the path, which we followed quickly to the hut.

The Dolomites no longer held any attraction for us that year, yet as we drove down from the Forcella Staulanza, the smiling fields lay invitingly blue with lavender flowering beneath dark fir trees. And Cortina d'Ampezzo, where we had to pick up our luggage, was overflowing with a noisy and cheerful crowd. But for us there was no stopping: we slept there one night, and were off again; we were at Bolzano by dinner-time, and by two in the morning at Turin, where we repacked our equipment and set off for Switzerland. The shores of Lake Maggiore . . . Arona . . . Stresa . . . Baveno . . . a smiling countryside crossed at high speed . . . gardens full of flowers overlooking the road . . . renewed temptations . . . gay groups of girls in summer frocks, which our rapid passage made even more attractive, for we were only allowed a first fleeting impression . . . boats with spotless sails furrowing the scarcely rippled surface of the lake . . . enchanting places, which called to us to stop. Why didn't we stop? Why all this feverish rushing from place to place as though we were chasing after lost happiness? Here was a corner of paradise which offered a haven to our storm-tossed ship, and within the harbour lay certain security, comfort, and a great deal else that most people hold dear. But already the ship's prow was headed for the open seas and the great storm winds.

After Domodossola, where we entered the harsh precipitous valley that leads to the Simplon, we felt as if we were moving from one world to another. Gradually the valley filled with shadow and the last light faded from the peaks. All was silent as we crossed the frontier and it was dark when we came to Gaudo, where we intended to spend the night. The bracing air of the near-by glaciers reawoke our enthusiasm: tomorrow we would have our axes in our hands again, and all our defeatist ideas would be blown away on the wind.

After a long and dusty drive across Switzerland we arrived next day at Grindelwald. At the hotel where we stopped and unpacked our sacks, ropes, and ironmongery, the porter asked with a wink, "North Face of the Eiger?" and went on to tell us that there were some German parties about in the district. However, the weather was anything but favourable.

Grindelwald is as bad a place as Chamonix for uncertain weather. We did just manage to catch a glimpse of the Eiger-wand between two falls of snow: it was wrapped in cloud, the upper half all white and the lower half darkened by water streaming ceaselessly down. So after three days we gave up our plan and went on to Chamonix to pursue our quest. There we found rain and snow, the Aiguilles were white right down to the two-thousand metre level (6,500 feet) and the north faces were like so many slabs of ice. We waited two days, and then irritably moved off again and headed south for the Dauphiné where, a year ago, the fates had been particularly kind to us.

One of the great walls that attracted us was the north face of the Ailefroide and it headed our programme. Conditions there were slightly better, and we lost no time in setting out on a reconnaissance. We made a careful study of the very complicated line of ascent up the middle of the wall; then we started up determinedly, to the accompaniment of whining stones, meaning to go only a short way before the clouds lying stationary at 13,000 feet should begin to discharge their rain and snow upon us. We climbed up 500 feet and then came down; but the following night a lot of snow fell here too, right down to 8,000 feet, and we realised that, this year, north faces were out of the question. We should have to fall back on some great south-facing ridge, which might still offer a chance of dry rock.

Our choice fell upon the south-east ridge of the Pic Gaspard (12,700 feet), one of the highest peaks in the Dauphiné. At about 10,000 feet this ridge suddenly surges up in a fantastic escarpment, yellow and vertical, that seizes the imagination. A third of the way up, the extraordinarily bold sweep of the ridge is interrupted by a horizontal section bristling with gendarmes; then it continues in great overhanging bluffs which peter out close to the summit. From a first cursory reconnaissance through field-glasses, it looked as if there were no break in the possible line of ascent except at one point about half-way up where an enormous tower stood out uncompromisingly.

We decided to attack as soon as the weather allowed; but it was a bad summer over most of Europe, with hurricanes and floods, and we had to put off our plan from day to day, while the snow accumulated on the ledges and in the deep-cut chimneys. Only the soaring crest and the great smooth, vertical bluffs on the ridge remained dry. During lulls in the bad weather we made some brief sorties from the hut, devoted to reconnaissance and edelweiss. Then storms would force us indoors again and we spent long hours lying on our palliasses, for the hut's one living room was bitterly cold. The bad weather showed no signs of breaking, and Lucien was due back in Paris on September 3. All hope of doing the climb began to disappear, and the patience of climbers like ourselves, not used to hurling themselves against impossible conditions, began to give out, and a desperate decision took shape in our minds: to have a shot the minute a break in the weather made it faintly possible. And so nearly ten days went by, during which we heard that two of the Germans whom we had seen at the foot of the Eiger had decided to make a bid for it, and had been killed on the wall, trapped up there for ever in an icy tomb.

At 10 o'clock on the morning of August 29 a violent northwest wind swept away all the clouds and suddenly a blazing hot sun began to melt the snow which had streaked the yellow walls with white. We decided to set out next day, but when the alarm sounded at 2 a.m. on the 30th, and we went out for a look, there was nothing but mist and hail. The filthy weather sent us back to bed, cursing; but when we got up again at 7 there was not a cloud in the sky!

We left the hut at 9, and it took us three hours to climb up the 3,000 feet to the foot of the rocks. At 12.45 we changed into espadrilles; usually on very difficult rock climbs nailed boots are left behind, but this time we should need them on the descent so they had to be added to our load; Lucien also put the collapsible ice-axe into his sack, and off we went. After three or four rope-lengths up hard slabs, we came to the first serious difficulty, a vertical blackish-coloured wall, exceedingly difficult, where we had to belay on pitons after each run-out, for there were no stances. A few more rope-lengths brought us to the top of the first steep step, and before us rose a long series of gendarmes. This was the horizontal part of the ridge and at the end, beyond two big gendarmes higher than the rest, the great yellow cliff we had spotted from below seemed to bar the way. We stopped a moment to look at it, and then continued rapidly along the precipitous and airy crest, which maintained a high standard of difficulty. While we were traversing one of the gendarmes and I was in a lay-back position in an open corner, my left foot slipped on a slimy hold and in a flash I swivelled round on my right foot and my left shoulder hit the other wall. At the same instant my right hand, with which I was pressing desperately against the rock, found a hold and I stopped myself. With an effort I regained my balance and climbed up, then paused and looked down at Lucien a hundred feet below. He was pale.

"Hullo! Can I come up?"

I grinned down at him. And so the gendarmes succeeded each other without interruption and for far longer than we had anticipated. There was only an hour of daylight left and we were still a long way from the steep step we had hoped to reach on the first day. We had in fact only done about a third of the climb. However we had to stop, for an hour doesn't take one very far, and bivouac sites were few and far between on the ridge. There was a convenient platform just here, six foot by three—true, it was covered with snow, but we paved it with large stones to make a nice soft mattress. It was a palace compared with the bivouac on the Jorasses. At 8 o'clock we crept into the Zdarsky tent, and during the night we were even able to indulge in the luxury of a short snooze. Friendly stars looked down on us from a clear sky.

At 7.45 a.m. we started off again, climbing slowly and laboriously: it took us nearly two hours and a half to reach the foot of the steep step. A first attempt to force a way straight up cost us over an hour before it petered out. Then we put on our nailed boots and went to have a look at the east flank, which was covered with snow and verglas. A long traverse on a snow-covered ledge brought us to a narrow wet chimney, which proved to be a very hard pitch indeed. After the chimney we climbed up for another 150 or 200 feet on broken rock covered with snow and verglas, where we moved with infinite caution. After this we were able to change back into espadrilles.

We had contoured round the obstacle, but the upper part of

the ridge still extended a long way ahead of us, and we could now see it was cut by two high vertical grey cliffs, invisible from below. It was nearly 1 o'clock and our stomachs were crying out for food, but we had few provisions left and still fewer hours of daylight, so we carried on without a meal, both feeling pretty anxious. Soon we came to the gap beneath the first grey cliff. We surveyed it rapidly: there was a possibility that we might be able to avoid it on the left, but this would have entailed climbing down the face for about 200 feet and then up again by a complicated line of ledges and little gullies to a point beyond which we could see nothing. It was more than likely that even there it wouldn't go, so the pitch would have to be forced direct. A third of the way up the cliff there was a slight depression on the left which gave some hope, but the wall was smooth, absolutely vertical and repulsive-looking, and we could only see ten or fifteen feet of it. Beyond that we should be on unknown ground. I climbed up for twenty feet or so, traversed well to the left and drove in a first piton, then crossed to the other side of the ridge, and lost sight of Lucien. Now I was on my own, and I could see the whole of the pitch. A few yards further on the rock became more broken; below me there was an overhang. I traversed two or three yards and put in another piton. I hesitated before starting; once embarked there would be no possibility of return. And if I were to fall, I should swing beneath the overhang and it would be impossible for Lucien to pull me up. It would mean a slow death, swinging in space. I waited a minute and looked up. How blue the sky was, up there!

Then I started. Stretching up as far as I could reach I managed to find some invisible holds. There was next to nothing for the feet, and the moves had to be made in rapid succession for the strain was too great to allow one to remain on the holds. Another yard to go. Three fingers of my right hand found a minute crevice on the left and, hanging from these three fingers, I swung my body out into space and with the tip of my left foot reached a slight protuberance on the edge of a slab. For the next three yards it was easier, and then I came to a stance. The whole operation had taken only a few minutes. So brief a moment in time, but crammed with a life-time of sensation. Overhead the sky was shining bluer than ever, just for me alone. I knocked in a piton and brought Lucien up. Then for 130 feet we went straight up, always on vertical rock, wonderfully sound but exceedingly difficult; we were now above the steep step.

But it was not yet finished. After we had gone along the ridge for a bit, it steepened again and took on an even more lowering aspect. There was no possibility of avoiding it either to right or left, for it was flanked by smooth vertical walls plunging down for thousands of feet. Either we should have to climb up its crest or else we were beaten. It was thirty hours since we had left the hut and on this second day we had scarcely stopped at all. Yet the hours had flown by, the sun was sinking inexorably towards the horizon, and a second bivouac seemed likely. Lucien remarked that the ordinary route, by which we would descend, was child's play: we should only need an hour to get down on to the glacier. So on we went, and as we approached the next steep step things looked more cheerful, for the ridge was split by a crack, and it seemed as though we ought to be able to make our way up it. I took off my sack and went straight to the attack. The difficulty was extreme, but not alarming, and this obstacle was quickly over-come. But though the main difficulties were then over, our goal was still distant. The outline of the ridge had lost its un-compromising appearance and become semi-horizontal, but it ran on with ups and downs for another thousand feet or so, and the summit was still invisible though we guessed it must lie behind a final shoulder. The way seemed to be bewitched —for hours and hours we had gone on in desperation, without drinking, without eating, without stopping, always with the illusion that it would end beyond the next gendarme. . . . But the goal kept on retreating before us like a will-o'-the-wisp.

We continued up the ridge for another couple of hours, then at last reached the summit at 7.30 and quickly took a look at the way we should have to go down. The easy route had vanished—the 700 feet to the glacier were covered with snow and verglas. Getting down would be hard work. And as there were only forty minutes of daylight left there was nothing for it but to prepare a second bivouac, my seventh of the season— good preparation for a rheumatic old age!

Lucien was worried by the look of the weather, for the sky had turned as red as the gates of hell and the snow-covered walls around us had taken on a strange colour, something between violet and a leaden grey. It was a lurid sunset, and we weren't at all cheered up by what it promised, so we set to work to prepare the bivouac. The summit blocks were wrenched from their places and their age-long quiet disturbed as we hurled them over the cliff where they bounded down with a noise of thunder. From the tiny shelter thus contrived, for hours we anxiously watched the changes in the sky. But the storm, which had seemed to be imminent, was slow to break, and in the morning the sun managed to shine through the mist.

At 8 o'clock we began the descent. Dead tired and dropping with sleep, it took us more than three hours to reach the glacier, which we descended like robots. We reached the hut at 3 o'clock, and returned to Grenoble next day.

Seven: 1936

First ascent of the north-west wall of the Ailefroide

THE programme we had drawn up for the summer season of 1936 was certainly not lacking in consistency.

As the major problems of the Olan, the north face of the Drus and the north face of the Grandes Jorasses had been solved in 1934 and 1935, our ambitions turned towards another trinity: the north face of the Eiger by the direct route, the "Walker" on the north face of the Grandes Jorasses, and the north face of the Ailefroide. This was a year not only of new goals, but also of new equipment: boots with cleated rubber soles (vibrams) to replace nails—an innovation which was very soon to revolutionise climbing technique in the Western Alps. Last year, on the Pic Gaspard, we had learnt what it was like to do a pure rock climb of over 3,000 feet with one's boots in the sack the whole way. I hoped that this year there would be no nailed boots and no espadrilles: I got Bramani to make me a pair of light-weight unlined boots, half-way between an espadrille and a boot.

On July 20 I went to Courmayeur and over the Col du Géant, on my way to meet Lucien Devies in Chamonix where, according to prevailing conditions, we would decide which expedition to do. While I was speeding down towards the Mer de Glace, highly pleased with my new light-weight boots, even on snow and ice, I met some Frenchmen who were being shepherded to the Torino hut by four guides. It was at a place where there was no alternative route through the icefall above the Requin hut, and I stood aside to let the first group pass. They were bristling with crampons and ropes, and looked at me with some surprise, as if wondering what on earth such an individual could be doing alone and in town boots all among the crevasses. One of the guides looked me up and down severely: "You've got the wrong kind of boots, Monsieur."

"Yes. I'm just out for a walk!"

And off I went at full speed, bounding over the crevasses, imagining the dreadful tales of my impending doom that the scandalised guides would tell their horrified clients.

In Chamonix, Lucien and I weighed things up. It didn't look like being a very good summer for big climbs. There was a lot of snow on the Pennines and the Graian Alps, and storms in Savoy—from the Montenvers I had been able to see that the Jorasses were white with snow and that there was nothing doing there. Things would certainly not be any better in the Oberland. Only the Dauphiné, being further south and less exposed to precipitation, left us some hope; so, on July 21, we left Chamonix for La Bérarde which we reached the same evening.

When Lucien Devies had spoken to me of the north-west face of the Olan two years before, he had—with all his expert knowledge of the Dauphiné and its unsolved problems—put this climb first on his programme. It was then considered, in French climbing circles, to be the greatest of the Dauphiné problems, not so much on account of its difficulty but because of the great size of the wall—over 3,000 feet high—and the total absence of any route on that side. On the Ailefroide, on the contrary, Dibona and Mayer, and the Vernet brothers, had forced routes up the immense bastion on the north side. Nonetheless the structure of this side gave ample justification for the view that the real wall, the north-west wall, still remained to be climbed. In fact the north side of the Ailefroide extends for nearly two miles and has two faces, north-east and north-west, either side of a central rib that faces due north.

The north-east wall is not so high, is more broken up, and has a large hanging glacier suspended on the face. The central spur or Costa Rouge ridge is a magnificent buttress supporting the massive structure of the mountain; it was climbed in 1911 by Guido Mayer with Angelo Dibona. The difficulties are not very great, but they are frequently accentuated by verglas.

The north-west wall, more than 3,000 feet high over a distance of about three-quarters of a mile, was still unclimbed. In 1929 the Vernet brothers had attacked the wall on the left, by a couloir raked by frequent stone-fall, which had brought them out on to the upper third of the Costa Rouge ridge. But this route in no way solved the central problem of the wall which remained entirely virgin. From the summit of the Olan, Devies had pointed out the Ailefroide to me in the distance and told me its Alpine history—until then I had never heard of it. The savage aspect of this great 3,000-foot precipice fired my imagination, and we immediately decided that our next visit to the Dauphiné should be devoted to the Ailefroide. It was a happy decision, for it turned out to be the finest climb we made in the district, and if from a technical point of view it does not reach the extreme limit of difficulty, it ranks nevertheless as one of the most interesting ascents in the Alps.

As we made our way early the next afternoon towards the Temple-Ecrins hut, we did not know if or when we should be able to get to work. But our sacks were loaded with several days' provisions and we had confidence in our lucky star, which had so far always smiled on us during our brief visits to these mountains.

The weather was still unsettled. High up in a heavily clouded sky, two winds were fighting for the ascendancy, with the north wind gaining ground. At a turn of the path, behind a hump at the end of the valley, our wall came into view; there it was, enormous, static, waiting beneath rolling clouds for us pygmies to attack. It was streaked with ice, but no snow lay on the vertical cliffs. Conditions were certainly better than the year before, and we felt that overpowering urge to get to grips with the problem which, whatever the undertaking, is the best guarantee of success. During this brief halt on the path, we decided without any hesitation that if the north wind prevailed for the next few hours we would start that same night.

After supper we went out to inspect the sky. There was not a cloud to be seen and the wind was in the right quarter, so we set our alarm for 2 a.m., and at 3 we left the hut. If successful, we should be descending on the other side, so that even if we were missing for a week no one would worry about us or wonder what had happened to us. Moreover there was no one in the whole district, neither climber nor guide, capable of forming a rescue party on so difficult a face. One of the privileges of mountaineering in the wild and unfrequented Dauphiné Alps, is that you have to rely entirely upon your own resources, and this brings a harsh pleasure with it, as though you really were exploring unknown country. And we were all the more appreciative of our relative solitude in that we had lately been on climbs where the bivouacs had been cheered by community singing and accordions from below!

Last year we had built a cairn to mark the point at which to leave the path and take to the steep scree-slopes which have to be crossed obliquely in order to reach the Costa Rouge glacier, and we had also made other cairns on the moraine during an afternoon's reconnaissance, but this year there was no moon and we had to rely entirely upon our instinct. We spotted the place by timing ourselves, leaving the path after forty minutes' walking.

Not far from the glacier we had to cross a small couloir filled with frozen gravel embedded in snow. I raised the lantern to look for the best way and saw a big boulder on which I leant as I went down without thinking for a moment that in this motionless mass the fates had concealed a trap. Although I had barely touched it the rock tipped over and fell behind me. To avoid it I jumped sideways, but in the dark I could not choose a footing on firm ground, and unfortunately slipped and pitched down the stones. I stopped myself on the snow and picked myself up, bruised and covered in blood. Devies came over to me and relit the lantern, which had gone out but which I was still clutching in my hand.

I made a rapid survey of the damage: my upper lip was split, three teeth were loose, and on my right side at the level of the lower ribs I felt a sharp pain which suggested a fracture; this was confirmed by a medical examination a few days later. I realised that if I decided to turn back I should not be able to do any more climbing that year. A wave of anger came over me at the thought of this stupid accident and, as so often at moments of disaster, I felt absolutely unperturbed. Everything that bound me to life was swept away by a fierce lust for action: the crazy exaltation of the fighter hurling himself regardless upon his opponent's weapon. A sudden urge, perhaps, but it was to last for fifty-six hours. Lucien realised that it would mean going through with it right to the summit unless we wished to remain on that vast wall for all eternity.

We went on into the night, and I pressed a piece of frozen snow against my battered face. By 6 o'clock we were at the foot of the climb; we crossed the bergschrund and continued upwards on ground we knew already. The pain in my side had decreased, but my mouth felt as though I was wearing a mask of iron. We came to the deep-cut couloir which slashes the wall diagonally; this was as far as we had gone during our reconnaissance the previous year, and we crossed it hurriedly on account of the frequent stone falls. We climbed up on the other side over verglas-coated rocks and then continued on easier ground for a few rope-lengths, to the point where the pillar that marked the line of our ascent on the lower section of the wall abruptly steepens into a vertical triangular-shaped cliff. After a brief examination we decided to try on the left, and the real difficulties began with the first chimney. We came out on to the crest of the pillar which soared skywards in a precipitous, dolomitic sweep, and forced our way up a dièdre, followed by a vertical crack which petered out on to a smooth forbidding-looking wall which I endeavoured to avoid on the left. But after ten feet, I had to come back. Round the far side of the pillar the wall became quite impracticable, falling in a single sweep to a shoot of glazed slabs raked by stonefall. So I attacked the wall direct: eighty feet of extremely difficult free climbing with practically no belays, and not until I was half-way up the pitch was I able to stop and put in a piton. Making a tremendous effort Devies succeeded in joining me, and after a traverse to the right, where we balanced over space, the difficulties eased up though they still remained of a very high order. Again higher up we had our work cut out to get up an extremely difficult dièdre. There followed an uninterrupted succession of steep narrowing walls, exposed traverses, elegant pitches, all very difficult, which finally brought us to the summit of the pillar.

From there onwards the whole aspect of the climb changed

completely. So far we had been confronted by 2,000 feet of sound rock, dry, dependable and sheltered from falling stones. Now the wall spread out before us: to begin with, there was a gigantic slab of grey, polished rock some 300 feet high which, when we had examined it through glasses the previous year, had revealed itself as the most unpredictable part of the climb; immediately afterwards there followed a series of red walls broken by ledges covered with frozen snow; the walls themselves were furrowed by chimneys which were lined with ice and glinted with verglas.

We halted below the narrow crest of snow that ran from the pillar up to the slab. In spite of the bodily pain which returned with any prolonged halt, I could not do other than pause to contemplate the horrific beauty of that giant wall which, from the airy ledge where we had stopped, could be seen in all its magnitude. Among the climbs I have done there are only two which can rival it in the sweep of its architecture: the north wall of the Civetta and the north face of the Grandes Jorasses. The Civetta is more powerful, and its immense organ-pipes give it greater harmony of line; the north face of the Jorasses is more savage and forbidding with its succession of icy slabs. The Ailefroide seemed to combine the characteristic features of both: vertical pillars dropping from the sky for hundreds of feet, vertiginous ice-slopes clinging by a miracle to the wall, great walls of warm-coloured rock tinged to flaming red by the sun, deep icy chimneys, ledges of ice.

An avalanche of stones thundered down on our right some distance away, but a splinter of rock the size of a hat bounded off the rock at an angle and headed in our direction, hit the rock again, bounced off, and came straight at us . . . Look out! It landed like a cannon-ball on the snow crest fifteen feet from where I stood, was slowed down by the layer of frozen snow, sprayed me with white from head to foot, and then passed eighteen inches from Devies' head. Grateful for the warning, we hastily did up our sacks and moved off. Very soon we were on the great grey slab—400 feet of continuous climbing of extraordinary difficulty (T.D. Standard), belaying on pitons with no stances. It was also the part of the climb that was most exposed to falling stones which repeatedly whined overhead. It was past 6 o'clock when we reached the large snow-ledge on the upper third of the wall. We still had two hours of daylight, but we did not know what was in store for us on the last part of the ascent, or whether it would be possible to bivouac. Nor could we make out exactly where we were. So we decided to go to the left and make for a platform which appeared to offer a convenient halting-place for the night. In three rope-lengths we were there, only to discover that, instead of the hoped-for platform, there was a dome of snow which only left free a small sloping ledge, two foot wide, at the foot of a rock wall. It couldn't be helped and there we stopped. We organised the bivouac as best we could, belaying ourselves to pitons and fixing the Zdarsky tent to the rock. By now the sun had disappeared behind a line of distant mountains, and the horizon was streaked with bands of dark red; the wind had got up and was blowing from the north, piercing cold, but an essential guarantee of fine weather. After a final friendly wave to that scene of our past battles, the Olan, now silhouetted black against a last faint gleam in the sky, we crept under our frail silken shelter. Huddled close together, we began the familiar bivouac routine: we took off our espadrilles, and stuck them in our rucksacks with our feet on top of them, and had a bite to eat. We were rather bothered by our physical condition. Because of insufficient training Lucien had felt his appendix a bit during the early part of the climb; he had gradually recovered, but was now feeling the effects of his efforts. And the first icy touch of the cold was enough to start my bruises hurting again.

In the morning we prepared our sacks slowly and it was 7 when we got back to the large snow-covered ledge, which we followed towards a tiny snow-filled gap. Then the struggle began, both with the verglas and with my ribs. I climbed slowly, feeling with the tip of my espadrille for the essential square half-inch of dry rock. At each step there was a stabbing pain in my side, so sharp that I had to grit my teeth to prevent myself from letting go. And every time I gritted my teeth, the three loose ones in the torn gum sent pains shooting through and through my head. But I had to climb on. Devies, on the other hand, had completely recovered.

Once at the gap we bore to the left; it was less difficult here, but not for long. We came to a depression and after a few rope-lengths we again met with vertical cliffs almost entirely covered with verglas. Nothing is more treacherous than this thin film of frozen water on the rocks which coats slabs, effaces holds, blocks up cracks. You get no grip with your espadrilles, and your hands freeze on contact with it. The nervous strain is increased even more than the actual technical difficulty, for you have to move with a total lack of security.

We went slowly, but the goal was getting nearer. Already above and to the right, the terminal ridge began to stand out and we were able to inspect the mountain's final defences. Ahead of us was a vertical reddish-coloured rib, topped with an enormous overhang; beyond it we sensed, rather than actually saw, the angle ease off. Perhaps this was the way out. Anyway, on with it! We soon came to the steep rib, which we by-passed on the left. Then the way was barred by a very severe little wall, leading to a chimney. I climbed it, putting in two pitons, but I had barely got into the chimney when Devies asked:

"Is there a way out?"

"I can't say yet—the chimney ends under the overhang."

In any case I would have to go on, and as soon as Devies had joined me, I continued. The chimney was full of ice and the walls coated with verglas. I gained height slowly, wedging my body across the chimney, and those movements with my legs wide apart so aggravated the pain in my side that I had to summon every ounce of strength not to give it all up and let myself go. After two rope-lengths I was at the overhang. On the left a slanting ledge ran up towards the sky, but to reach it there was a traverse over the abyss, on friable rock and extremely difficult. Then along the ledge for another forty feet and, at last, I was up. I stopped, and Devies joined me. Another couple of rope-lengths over progressively easier ground brought us to the summit at 3 p.m.

We stopped for an hour to bask in the sun, and at 4 o'clock

we began the descent. But although the shadows were lengthening in the Sélé valley we were quite incapable of hurrying. There was still an hour of daylight left when the last rappel deposited us on the snow slope. We crossed the bergschrund without bothering to belay each other; on the soft snow of the bridge where I was floundering about on all fours, the tracks made by Devies, now walking on ahead, had left holes through which I could glimpse blue depths which at any other time would have given me the shivers. We ran down the glacier— or at least I thought we were going down—but night caught us wandering about among the crevasses.

We tried to bear to the right towards a rib of rock outlined in the last gleams of daylight; we sank into the snow, sometimes above our knees, without knowing whether we were breaking through into hidden crevasses, or merely sinking into drifts blown up by the wind. Finally we were brought to a halt by an ice slope on which we could not venture in the dark with only one axe, so we retraced our steps, resigned now to a second bivouac. We scraped up some snow with the axe to make a flat space on which we laid the rope, then we sat down with the Zdarsky over the top of us. Nothing to eat; nothing to drink; only an icy wind which pierced right through us and set the tent flapping.

On the morning of the 25th we were utterly spent, and I could scarcely move. We packed up our sacks in a squall of hail, then staggered down to the bottom of the glacier. At 10.30 we reached Ailefroide, fifty-six hours after leaving the Temple-Ecrins hut.

Eight : 1936

Christmas: solo ascent of the Matterhorn from the Italian side

Two months of forced immobility were enough to make me forget the rough time the Ailefroide had given us; so much so that at the end of September I had begun to climb again on the rocks of our Turin training-ground. All that remained of our great adventure in the Dauphiné was a memory tinged with regret, but with return to my usual form came the renewed urge to tackle some major enterprise. It looked as if the coming winter might be particularly favourable for big ascents. But I knew both from my own experience and that of others, that the best moment for these winter trips is generally in February, and I made no definite plans for the immediate future. Meanwhile I devoted my Sundays to expeditions on skis.

On the morning of December 20, with my friends P. Ceresa, Fiorio and Poma, I went by car up to Breuil. Our objective was the Breithorn, a four-thousander well known to skiers from Turin, which the new Plan Maison cable-railway made it possible to do comfortably in the day. While we were climbing up the glacier above the Col du Théodule my gaze frequently strayed to the Matterhorn. In the pure cold atmosphere of a December day, this "noblest death-trap in Europe" was like a sleeping giant crouched on the edge of the vast snowy wastes of the Breuil amphitheatre. From time to time avalanches thundered down from the hanging glaciers; a long period of fine weather, with a series of violent gales, had cleared the snow from the steep rocks. Only on the Pic Tyndall, a faint white line betrayed the presence of a cornice.

During a halt I exchanged a few remarks with my friends: "It looks to me as if one might get up . . ." But I said nothing of the plan that was slowly taking shape in my mind. I had not then climbed the Matterhorn from the Italian side and I felt myself powerfully impelled towards adventure into the unknown. And this desire was accompanied by that peculiar state of mind which precedes action, when every nerve and every muscle vibrates in unison, when, urged on by some imperious necessity, one's whole being longs for battle, for the exhilarating breath of danger, and for difficulties to tackle and to overcome.

I returned to Turin in the evening anxiously turning over my idea and longing to be already up there on the heights. Next afternoon, after I had prepared my rucksack, I went out into the streets of the town to let my excitement cool off a bit in the open air. Almost automatically I walked up to the viewpoint on the Monti dei Cappuccini. I heard the call of the distant wind which had cleared the air at sunset, and tinged the horizon with green. Two little clouds above the Gran Paradiso caught the last rays of the sun, while the first lights appeared in the town below. The thought of approaching action aroused strange and contradictory sensations in me. I felt an immense pity for all the little men who toiled on in the prison which society has succeeded in building against the open sky; who knew nothing and felt nothing of what I knew and felt at that moment. Yesterday I was like them, and in another few days I would be like them again. But today I was a prisoner set free; and tomorrow I would be a lord and master, a commander of life and of death, of the stars and of the elements.

Back in the town again I wandered aimlessly through the streets, packed with cheerful crowds getting ready to celebrate Christmas. Mothers and children went by with their arms full of parcels, and a girl brushed against me and smiled. Faint now was the call, drowned in the city's hum and noise, and a strange nostalgia rose up from the depths of my heart, and redoubled the joy I felt at my approaching farewell to this world.

At Breuil, on Tuesday the 22nd, I looked for a porter to save me the effort of carrying my sack during the first part of the ascent on skis, and found Marco Pession of Valtournanche. I told Graziano Bich, manager of the hotel of that name, of my plans and at 8.15 on the morning of the 23rd the porter and I took the Plan Maison *téléférique* which gave us a start of 2,000 feet.

We reached the Carrel cross at 10.20; Pession came on for another half-hour and then I took my sack and continued alone.

At the foot of the Matterhorn glacier I left my skis, which were no longer any help, and continued on foot, sinking wearily into the snow at each step. By 12.30 I had reached the berg-schrund at the foot of the couloir coming from the Col du Lion, and here I put on my crampons. This was the decisive moment, and I could not help feeling apprehensive. Formidable before me rose the Matterhorn, with all its legends, all its tragedies. Marco Pession was already far away, gliding down on his skis towards the new winter resort of Cervinia. Above me were snow and ice, rock and solitude; I felt very near to wishing for a companion, but then I reflected how far finer a struggle it would be alone. After a last look at my crampon-straps, I tackled the bergschrund. Very, very slowly, I moved up, look-ing for the spot where the bridge seemed strongest; I prodded it with my axe—it was soft and not very thick. I climbed up, established myself on a block of ice and stuck my axe into the opposite lip of the schrund as high up as possible. Then I jumped, and hauled myself up; I was across. In the couloir the snow was soft and I climbed up without stopping, making deep tracks—a very exhausting business.

I reached the Col du Lion at 1.45, stopped for something to eat and moved off again at 2.30. The rocks up to the Luigi Amedeo hut were dry, with only here and there a few patches of ice where I had to cut steps, and at 3.40 I arrived at the airy shelter, an eagle's nest perched under a tower, over 12,600 feet up on the formidable south-west ridge of the Matterhorn.

I spent the evening getting ready for the next day. I felt absolutely calm and confident; I was splendidly fit, and not in the least overtired by the exertions of the first part of the ascent. At 7.30 I settled down in the blankets; when I got up twelve hours later, on the morning of the 24th, my pocket thermometer registered 16° Fahrenheit inside the hut. The cold, therefore, was not too intense. At 8 o'clock I went outside, but the sun was not yet up, so I waited another half-hour before starting.

On the 100 feet of fixed rope which one has to climb my hands grew numb at once, although I kept on my gloves.

From time to time I slapped them against my thighs to get some feeling back into them and continued climbing as far as the Linceul, a patch of névé, which one has to cross diagonally. It was here that my friend Crétier and two others had fallen, when returning from making a new route on the Pic Tyndall in treacherous snow conditions—a memory which certainly did nothing to encourage me. I tried the snow: it was very bad—soft, with ice underneath. I preferred to try higher up on the rocks—even if they should prove more difficult—by a slightly ascending traverse. In this way I avoided the first part of the snow slope, but it was not possible to get round the upper half in the same way. Standing in a rather awkward position, I put on my crampons, got down on to the snow and traversed slowly across, carefully pressing my foot down each time until the points of my crampons bit into the ice underneath. Then I took to the rocks again, and after climbing up two fixed ropes got back on to the ridge. I followed it, keeping a bit on the west side which was in shadow and consequently still icy, climbed up steep rock walls, cut steps on patches of ice and in frozen gullies, and so arrived under the Pic Tyndall. Here the ridge evens out into a sort of hog's back, without any steep steps. I thought the snow up there might hold, and I put my crampons on again. It was a highly dangerous place; the ridge narrowed to a thin crest, and the snow was powdery with a light wind-crust. I knew from the first step that it was most unsafe, and neither with crampons nor ice-axe could I get any purchase. I progressed in the manner of a tight-rope walker, balancing along between two precipices of more than 3,000 feet with absolutely no security. When the angle lessened and the crest became almost horizontal, I forgot all about style and dignity and straddled the ridge, helping myself along with my feet acting as paddles, in the same way that children bestride sea-monsters in a swimming pool! The powder-snow flew up into the air and, just to make things pleasant, the wind blew it back into my face and down my neck.

At the shoulder the snow improved and I was able to resume a normal position. But I was by now nearly an hour behind schedule, and with the days being so short I realised that I should have my work cut out to get back in daylight. Every minute counted and for a moment I felt disheartened. I looked over towards the Col Félicité: the first steep step and the Enjambée were in execrable condition, all plastered with snow. I should lose more time there . . . perhaps I'd be wise to return to the hut and try again next day with the tracks already made.

So I turned back. But after a dozen steps I was brought up short by the sight of the crest which I had straddled, and the cornices of the shoulder. It would mean crossing these places three times more, multiplying the risks. One might just as well tackle the last part of the descent by moonlight. So again I turned about, crossed the Col Félicité and attacked the slope beneath the Tête du Cervin. Up above I could see the Jordan rope-ladder, and this normally easy bit was covered with ice. As I was obliged to move continually from rock to ice I took off my crampons and used my axe. It was a case of trying first one way, then another, and I made some slight variations in the route, and also lost time, so I forced the pace a bit, although I was beginning to tire. When I came to the ropes beneath the ladder, I was in luck, for they were dry: I climbed up the ladder, but at the top I had a nasty surprise. The slab above was covered with snow, and both the fixed rope and the stanchion to which it was attached were completely buried. Now, as I stood on the topmost rung, hanging right out in space, began some really interesting work. I took my axe out of my rucksack and began to hack away at the ice round the fixed rope; finally, foot by foot, I succeeded in freeing it altogether. When I had finished, my hands were frozen and I stopped a moment to restore the circulation. Then practically running along the now easier ridge, I reached the summit in a few minutes, at 2.10. My eyes circled the horizon. A whole world lay beneath me: mountain upon mountain, from Monte Rosa to the Bernese Oberland, from the nearby Täschhorn, Weisshorn and Dent Blanche to the giant Mont Blanc and its massif, and then, further away, to the Dauphiné and Monte Viso, gradually fading to distant shades of blue. The plain was hidden in mist.

But time pressed, so I put a note in the box beneath the

triangulation point, swallowed a few lumps of sugar and some prunes and then at 2.20 started down. I had little more than three hours of daylight left, and I sped down the ropes and the ladder, managed, not without difficulty, to negotiate the slabs again below the Tête du Cervin, crossed the Enjambée and so found myself back on the Pic Tyndall. There the tracks of my ascent helped me a bit—and anyway I had no time for any doubts. On the ridge below, I was able to avoid two of the ice pitches by roping down. I came to the Linceul just as the sun was disappearing. In the uncertain twilight I could not go down the way I had come up, and with infinite care I descended the whole length of the exposed slope.

Night had fallen, but the moon was nearly full and gave light enough to see by. Gusts of icy wind blew round me as I traversed beneath the Great Tower, and from a ledge I caught sight of a gleam a few hundred feet below: the roof of the hut. As I was going down the last of the fixed ropes I knocked the point of my axe, which I had stuck under the straps of my sack, violently against the rock. It slipped out from the straps and shot down into the black depths of the west face, sending out a shower of sparks where it first struck the rocks. However I couldn't stop then to think about this piece of bad luck: there would be time for that tomorrow. A few more yards and I was at the hut, at 6.15, with the lights of Breuil twinkling in the valley below.

I had eaten nothing all day, and as soon as I was inside I heated up some food on a providential spirit-stove; as it was Christmas Eve I crowned the feast by swallowing some hot water in which I had boiled a dozen prunes. Then I went outside for a moment. A strong cold wind had got up, and in the moonlight the mountains all around looked so unreal, so illusory, that I felt I was living in a dream-world, an actor in some marvellous children's story. A wave of melancholy swept over me; but the rumble of a sérac falling from the north face of the Dent d'Hérens brought me down to earth, and I went back into the hut and crawled under the blankets.

All night long the gale blew, and it was still going strong in the morning. I went out at about 9 o'clock, but the icy wind sent me scurrying back to wait until the sun had gained some strength. Meanwhile I searched for something to take the place of my lost ice-axe, but all I could find was the handle of the broom which, sharpened to a point, could be used as a staff. It wouldn't be much use, but in the couloir I should need some sort of support.

At 10.30 I began the descent. The gale, which was still blowing, had covered all the slabs with a coating of frozen sleet which made everything very dangerous. I went down with great care, roping down wherever possible. When I came to the tracks leading up to the Col du Lion I used crampons, and the snow was so soft that my broomstick was the greatest help. Crossing the bergschrund was easier going down, and on the glacier I followed my old tracks back to my skis. Slowly—for I was in no hurry—I let myself be carried valleywards. Above Plan Torrette I saw two skiers coming up towards me, and I immediately pointed my skis in their direction. The dream was over.

Nine: 1937

Requin by the Mayer-Dibona route—North face of the Petit Dru

AUGUST 1937 brought Devies and myself once more to Interlaken. We were out of training, and counted on getting fit in the district; but it looked as though the Eiger had signed a contract with the bad weather, and after a week in a hotel we went over to Chamonix. There, too, the weather was unsettled, but this did not prevent us from spending some pleasant days with a number of our friends of the Groupe de Haute Montagne.

While waiting for a good opportunity to repeat the north face of the Petit Dru, we climbed the Requin by the Dibona route: a most delightful climb, to be recommended to anyone who wants to go up this celebrated Aiguille. Near the top, completely carried away by enthusiasm for the climb, I tackled a formidable hundred-foot crack which turned out to be extremely hard. Thus, quite by mistake, I made a variation, and one to be avoided, unless the climber particularly wishes to indulge in a grade VI pitch. On our way back from the Requin we stopped at the Montenvers.

The north face of the Drus is one of the great climbs in the Western Alps. All those who are familiar with the Mont Blanc massif know the bold pyramid whose west wall rises in a precipitous sweep of virgin rock above the Mer de Glace.[1] The classic route on the south side is equally well known and figures largely in Alpine literature. The north face itself can easily be seen from below and the characteristic "Niche", a patch of snow set half-way up in the face like a precious stone, arouses the wonder of the crowds which the little Montenvers train disgorges all summer long. These tourists get a thrill of pleasure at touching the ice of the Mer de Glace, and give themselves the

[1] The west wall was climbed in 1952 by Guido Magnone, Beradini, Dagory and Lainé. The third ascent was made by a British party of two—Joe Brown and Don Whillans—in 1954. [*Translators' Note.*]

159

shivers on the *mauvais pas* a hundred yards from the hotel. But the cirque enclosed by the wall of the Drus and by the great slopes of the Aiguille Verte contains a world of terrifying beauty that cannot even be imagined from the Montenvers. Yet, close as it is to one of the most frequented places in the Alps, this cirque is known to only a very few climbers, for all the ascents there are of a high standard of difficulty.

There are three routes up the Aiguille Verte from here: one made by the brothers Gugliermina and Canzio, and two routes made by parties led by Armand Charlet. Attempts had been made on the north face of the Petit Dru by Franz Lochmatter, and there was the daring descent by Gréloz and Roch, who roped down this face and reported that it looked impossible to climb; there was also a desperate attempt by two young Austrians who fell to their death at the foot of the rocks. Finally, in 1935, after another abortive attempt by Lambert, came the great victory of the French pair Allain and Leininger, undoubtedly the finest French partnership of the time.

So we were particularly keen to climb this wall, but our first attempt had to be abandoned in the rain 300 feet from the start. The way up to the foot of the climb has nothing very nice about it, and takes time. From the Montenvers you go down to the Mer de Glace, traverse right across it and then climb up more than 4,500 feet of steep grassy slopes, long moraines and finally a short snow slope. On the strength of his special equipment, Allain bivouacked a certain distance up the wall, and spent two nights in the open. But we preferred comfortable beds and a night approach.

A week after our first attempt, we again left the Montenvers at 1 a.m. and by 5 o'clock we were at the foot of the snow slope. There we realised that we had made a big mistake in reducing our ice and snow equipment to one ice-axe, and no crampons. A week ago the slope had been covered with a thin layer of snow which had enabled our light-weight boots to get a grip, but this layer had now disappeared leaving bare ice. So we were forced to cut steps the whole way up the slope, which meant a considerable expenditure of energy, and above all a loss of time which resulted in a most uncomfortable bivouac after the climb. Our advice to parties repeating this route is to take crampons, one ice-axe being quite enough in any case.

At 7.30 we reached the rocks where we allowed ourselves a brief rest, and left again at 8 o'clock, two hours behind schedule. At first we climbed on easy rocks then, bearing to the right, up some rather tiring verglas-coated chimneys and cracks; an exposed traverse brought us out beneath the Niche. By a difficult crack which widened into a couloir-chimney we gained the sloping névé which covers the lower part of the Niche. We crossed this at its narrowest, going up obliquely from left to right, and making for the steep ridge separating the north and west faces. We continued up this ridge until it merged into the vertical wall, and it is here that the hardest climbing occurs. There is a succession of cracks with rounded edges, reached by a leftwards traverse, which slash the smooth walls for 130 feet or so, where the difficulties are continuous. However, enough pitons had been left in on the first and second ascents to lessen the original severity. I even managed to avoid using two or three of them. All the same, the climbing here is of absolutely first-class standard, and extremely tiring. Afterwards some easier sections alternate with some short very hard pitches where one has to throw in every ounce. However the climb has one general feature: there are plenty of ledges everywhere which allow one to belay and to rest comfortably, and this makes it a very safe climb. When, towards the end, the angle of the wall relents, the ascent ceases to be a pure rock climb, and alternates between bands of steep ice and broken rock; as there was a good deal of verglas we had to proceed with the utmost caution. Darkness overtook us when we were still battling with the final slopes; we despaired of reaching the summit and looked for a bivouac site under the terminal arête.

It was 9 p.m. when we came to a curious grotto of crystal, not more than a yard high, its bed formed of absolutely pure green ice. It was splendid to look at, but the prospect of spending a whole night there was quite definitely repellent. We were little more than a hundred feet from the summit, but it was pitch dark and it would have been risky to go on. So we resigned ourselves to the unpleasant prospect of a long vigil sitting on bare ice, on which we spread the ropes and our sacks. To add to the icy cold of our couch, a draught blew up from the back of the grotto. We tried in vain to sleep, reciting a *mea culpa* for not having brought our crampons, which would have enabled us to continue the climb, and enjoy a romantic bivouac on the classic site on the Petit Dru, described at length by Guido Rey and Charles Gos.

In the morning, when we made up our minds to get out of our bivouac tent, we saw a gleam of light at the back of the grotto where the draught came from. Much intrigued, I crawled on all fours towards the narrowing depths of the cave, and managed to wriggle along the crack. Suddenly, to my surprise I came out on to the vast terraces of the south face of the mountain, in the full light of the sun which was climbing up above the Aiguille de Leschaux! Had we discovered this tunnel the evening before we would have had a more comfortable bivouac. Lucien passed the sacks through to me and then followed himself, and after warming ourselves a bit in the sun we carried on to the summit.

The descent of the Petit Dru is rather long. At least so it seemed to us, for we were very weary, mostly because we had not been able to rest during the night. On the interminable steep moraines below the Charpoua hut, which are even more tiresome to go down than to come up, we met Lagarde and his party who were on their way to do the traverse of the Drus. Having heard about our proposed ascent, our friends had kindly thought of bringing up some beer which they now offered us with some other very welcome delicacies. And as we said goodbye, we made a date to meet them down in Chamonix.

Ten: 1938

In 1938 I was more determined than ever to tackle the problem of the Eiger. The mountain was in a fair way to becoming a regular obsession owing to the desperate assaults of German climbers. Characteristically, one party after another flung themselves at it, often technically incompetent or with insufficient training, caring little about their losses provided somebody eventually succeeded. But alas, my determination did not coincide with the possibility of leaving my work; I had to wait a long time, content to be all ready to grasp the opportunity when it came.

So, Lucien Devies not being available, I made arrangements with Gabriele Boccalatte. He had more spare time than I had, and early in July he went to Courmayeur; he had instructions to telegraph me when he considered conditions were possible; we would then meet at Aosta whence we would go on by car over the Great St. Bernard to Grindelwald. Meanwhile I would step up my training by making expeditions at top speed on Sundays with Gigi and Nicola Bottinelli. The best of these climbs was Boccalatte's direct route on the east face of the Aiguille de la Brenva. We left Turin by car on the Saturday afternoon and arrived the same evening at the Pavillon du Mont Fréty. On Sunday morning at 3 o'clock we left the Pavillon, and at 7 o'clock started up the wall. We reached the summit at 2.30 and were down in the valley by evening and able to start work again at 9 on Monday morning in Turin.

Meanwhile the days went by and no telegram arrived: a sign that conditions were still bad. But what did come, at the end of July, was the news that the Eigerwand had been conquered by two German parties led by Heckmair, in spite of bad weather and bad conditions. So our programme had to be altered and I wrote to Gabriele accordingly, telling him I would be taking my holiday about mid-August and asking him if he was agreeable to an attempt on the Walker spur on the north face of the Grandes Jorasses. He replied that he was, and that he awaited my arrival.

I left for Courmayeur on August 13. At Entrèves I learned that Boccalatte had gone to do the Innominata ridge of Mont Blanc, and that two days before Cassin and his party had gone over the Col du Géant. I was rather put out by both these items of news, for it was easy to guess that Cassin's objective was the very same as our own.

Determined to be on the spot myself, I went down to Courmayeur again to look for a guide who would be willing to follow me. Arthur Ottoz, then one of our best guides in the Western Alps and an absolutely first-class rock climber, was attracted by the idea, and in spite of the late hour we set out for the Col du Géant where we arrived at 11 p.m. The Torino was completely full and we had to spend the night on the benches of the living-room. It was not until 4 a.m. that two bunks were vacated and we were able to get a few hours' rest. At 8 o'clock, however, we were up again and making our way down the glacier towards the Requin hut and on to the Leschaux.

Unfortunately the weather had been fine for three days, and we supposed that the climbers from Lecco would already be on the face. Sure enough, on the Leschaux glacier we met Guido Tonella, who told us that Cassin, Esposito and Tizzoni had started on the climb the morning before and, after bivouacking a third of the way up the wall, were continuing towards the summit.

I realised that, as in 1935 with the Germans, the game was up. But it was my own fault, or anyway the fault of the atmosphere which had surrounded the Grandes Jorasses at that time. I had been too hesitant, I had insisted too much on absolutely settled weather and perfect conditions, and so from year to year I had put off the final assault. It was logical, therefore, that a party like Cassin's, which was free from the apprehen-

sions inspired by the scene itself, should—given its strength—
decide to tackle it straight away. In fact, the Lecco party had
never seen the Leschaux cirque before. I myself had obtained
similar results in the Dauphiné, on mountains of which I had
no previous knowledge. So I couldn't really complain.

We reached the hut at 11 a.m., but were unable to spot the
position of the party on the face. We had lunch and then
decided to go on in spite of the fatigue of a long approach
which, speaking for myself, had begun in Turin, and the effects
of which were now making themselves increasingly felt. The
weather, however, was changing. The wind was in the west
and thick mist had begun to form on Mont Blanc. At 2.30 we
were at the foot of the wall and from there we succeeded in picking out the other party, already high up on the great face. We
hailed each other, though only briefly, for the mist, which was
creeping down from the summit, soon hid them from sight. By
4.30 we had reached the foot of the great dièdre, the first serious
obstacle encountered by Cassin and overcome with the help of
a great many pitons. Now it was our turn to be enveloped in
mist, and sleet began to patter on our hoods. We realised then
that our efforts were useless. The Lecco party, in view of the
height they had reached, would have to force a way to the summit at all costs, but for us to start off with almost the entire
climb still ahead, and the immediate prospect of a snowfall,
would have been madness. So, after waiting for half an hour we
went down, and darkness fell long before we reached the
Leschaux hut.

The disappointment of missing this climb, undoubtedly the
greatest in all the mountains of Europe, was softened by the
fact that victory had gone to Riccardo Cassin. Cassin was born
a native of the Frioul, but when he was still quite young he
moved to Lecco for professional reasons, and Lecco adopted
him. He was certainly one of the most representative figures of
modern mountaineering—though possibly not as brilliant as
some others; his particular strength was his determination. The
secret of the German successes lies in their contempt of risk and
danger, and their over-estimation of their own powers. There
are plenty of them; many of them fall by the way, but many

succeed. But one doesn't often meet a German leader who succeeds on a number of major climbs over any length of time. After a great climb they just disappear, and there is another man, held in reserve, to take his place. To Italians, this way of living dangerously appears inhuman. The secret of Cassin's great victories lay in his thorough training—it was easy for him to start his season in the spring, in the nearby Grignetta group —in his clear and impartial estimate of his own capacity, and in a quite exceptional technique. He was a man who, once the goal had been settled, never turned back. Comici and the Dimai brothers climbed the north wall of the Cima Grande di Lavaredo in several stages, climbing up so far, then down again. Cassin would have remained on the wall for a week, but he would have got up. Once, when he was on the north wall of the Cima Ovest di Lavaredo, it began to rain shortly after the terrible traverse. Anyone else would have turned back and waited for fine weather. But Cassin kept on, clinging to the wall for three days and two nights, and won through. Another time, when he was caught in a severe storm on the north-east wall of the Piz Badile, he just kept going, and brought up not only his own party but also two climbers from Como, Molteni and Valsecchi, who had tacked on to him part of the way up the climb; they both died of exhaustion on the way down.

Other climbers might be more brilliant: Comici, for example, and Soldà. Comici climbed for pleasure, both physical and intellectual, and thought little of the actual objective. Cassin was more single-minded: he knew precisely what he wanted to do and the enterprise was completely identified with the objective. For Comici, climbing was an end in itself; for Cassin, a means to an end. One cannot judge Comici only by his ascents; on that showing, many climbers would be rated higher. But Cassin, on the contrary, should be judged on his achievements, and from this angle he need fear no comparison. He found a series of exceptional climbing partners—like Ratti, Esposito, Tizzoni—who always gave him splendid support, especially Ratti, who had himself successfully led some formidable climbs both in the Dolomites and in the Mont Blanc massif.

So I welcomed my countrymen's victory—not without some

regret, but certainly with no ill-feeling. Again I crossed the
Col du Géant back to Courmayeur, where at last I met Boccalatte. We cheered each other up over our setbacks, and began
to look around for a climb which would come up to the high
standard of our requirements.

With the fall of the north face of the Eiger and the Walker
spur, mountaineering in the Western Alps had come to a turn-
ing-point. These two great problems had been the object of
competition on the part of five nations, and had resulted in
one win for the Germans and one for the Italians. There did
not now seem to be any other wall whose ascent would constitute a problem big enough to warrant its becoming an object
of competition on a national scale. So mountaineering once
more became a personal and individual affair, and a new
route the private creation of the climber.

In the Western Alps there were still about thirty, perhaps
more, of these extremely difficult climbs. In the Mont Blanc
massif, there was one on the wall above the Fresney glacier,
springing from the Peuterey ridge and counterbalancing the
immense pillar of the Aiguille Noire: this was the south-south-
west face of the Picco Gugliermina. It surges up from a chaotic
sea of ice in a 2,600 foot sweep, triangular in shape and
strangely reminiscent of the Petit Dru seen from the Montenvers. Boccalatte had already made a reconnaissance the
previous year with Castiglioni, and had returned with the
impression that, although very hard, it ought to be possible. So
this, at Boccalatte's suggestion, was now the climb we chose.

On the Wednesday evening we foregathered at the Gamba
hut, and at 2 a.m. on Thursday, taking advantage of the moonlight, we made our way towards the foot of the climb. We
crossed the Col de l'Innominata to the chaotic Fresney glacier.
It was slow work through the séracs, though not tiring, and it
took us five hours to reach the ledge at the foot of the climb—
an hour more than we had estimated, on account of a very
wide jagged crevasse which barred our way 150 feet below the
ledge. It was possible to get round this crevasse on the left by
going much higher up, but I persisted in looking for a way
across on the right which would take us more directly to the

start of the climb. Gabriele followed me for a while without much conviction, then, more wisely, put on his crampons and, as we were not roped, went off by himself to cross on the left. Displaying a most culpable obstinacy, I succeeded in getting myself stuck on the steep edge of the crevasse, and since I had left my crampons behind at the hut, I had the unpleasant job of cutting steps. When I came to the place which I had thought looked possible from below, I found that I should have to make a jump about ten feet down and six feet across. Meanwhile Gabriele, having side-stepped the obstacle, was traversing rapidly along the rock.

I got into position on the edge and made two or three of those hesitating movements a little dog makes when, put down on a table too high for its liking, it cannot make up its mind to jump. In fact the crevasse did now appear wider, so I tried a psychological experiment: I hurled my ice-axe like a javelin to the other side, so that I should be obliged to go and fetch it. But I still couldn't bring myself to try it. My sack felt too heavy, so I threw that across too, but it did the dirty on me and rolled below the ice-axe, coming to rest lower down on a bridge which cracked in a far from reassuring manner. Clearly I was now for it: there was no longer any alternative. So, putting my jumping to the test, I landed on all fours on top of my ice-axe. I climbed down and retrieved my sack, and then joined Gabriele who had already reached the foot of the climb and was beginning to be funny at my expense—for my antics were not what one expects from any self-respecting mountaineer.

At 7.15 we left our ice-axes and started up the rock. The first few yards were easy, and Boccalatte had no hesitation on this already familiar ground. At 8.30 we halted on a ledge in order to examine the wall which now steepened to the vertical. It was split by a smooth curving crack, but as that was broken by overhangs we decided against it. On the right, a rounded rib ran up to the summit in one unbroken sweep, and as it looked better provided with holds, we made our way across to it by an ascending traverse. Now the difficulties increased progressively. For a couple of rope-lengths we climbed on a compact type of rock with rounded holds where it was hard to drive in pitons for belaying. Then the holds improved, but the climb became increasingly steep and strenuous. There were no stances, and after each run out we had to stop on very small holds and belay on pitons.

We climbed an extremely difficult and tiring crack by a lay-back. Then followed a flake some fifteen feet high and a foot thick which we climbed by back-and-knee up the chimney which separated it from the wall. At the top we sat on the edge of the flake with our backs to the void, thinking that we should be able to stop for a bit—it was 1 o'clock and we would have liked to eat something. But hardly had we settled down when Boccalatte thought he heard a crack. This had the effect of a cry of "Fire!" in a cinema. We tried to make ourselves as light as possible, and I went on up the wall on my right.

Other overhanging cracks followed upon each other, and the wall became even smoother and more forbidding. In one place I came to a halt for there were just no more holds, and the last belay piton was thirty feet below me. I remained where I was for a few minutes, hoping to find a crack, no matter how small, into which I could insert a piton. But there was nothing. Above me on the left, and about five feet away, I could see a good hold and I decided to try to reach it. I moved up with immense care, just keeping my balance, and got to within eighteen inches, then I was no longer in balance and had to move down. I tried again, twice, three times, first one way, then another, but I was still eight inches from the hold; I stretched out despairingly—only four inches now—but I knew I should come off so I prudently withdrew. Well, this looked like the end, for there was still 100 feet between us and the tower, which I could see above my head, and behind which presumably lay the big ledge under the summit. Beneath us the wall dropped for 2,000 feet and more—a delightful prospect to think of climbing down all that!

I looked down, but could see only ten foot of rope which then disappeared, under the overhang. Looking up I caught sight of a wrinkle behind the rounded edge of the ridge. I climbed down about a yard, leant out from the rock and changed feet hanging over space. Behind the ridge there was a crevice; in went a piton until it rang clear, then, holding the rope clipped to the piton with a karabiner, I was able to move to the left. I got a second piton into the wall, repeated the manœuvre, and reached a hold a couple of yards further on. Afterwards it went all right. The piton, which at the critical moment had given us the key to the climb, was left in position with the karabiner to enable Boccalatte to make the traverse, and also for the benefit of those who might wish to repeat this splendid climb.

We now bore to the right, still meeting great difficulties, until we reached a chimney-crack up which we climbed. At 4 o'clock we were on the ledge. For seven solid hours we had not been able to rest; now at last we could eat. But after half an hour we were off again, for the climb was not yet finished— far from it—there was still unknown ground ahead. The overhanging wall above us was split by a chimney. It seemed doubtful whether it was climbable, so we made a cast to the right for a couple of rope-lengths. Nothing doing there, either.

We climbed back and went to have a look on the other side. The ridge bounding the wall, here very narrow, looked more hopeful, but the question was how to reach it. The traverse was impossible by free climbing; the only hope lay in rope manœuvres. Retracing our steps, we picked out a slightly protruding spike of rock in the middle of the wall and climbed up it to gain some height. From this point we could try to reach a narrow platform fifty feet lower down and thirty feet further to the left. We arranged a rope loop, unroped and tied our two ropes together. Then I roped down and tried to swing across. But owing to the shape of the wall and the great distance, all my attempts were in vain. I stopped above one of the detached vertical flakes on the wall and tried to pass the rope behind it so as to get a closer take-off. But during the manœuvre the rappel rope slipped off my shoulder and jumped clear of the flake. I then found myself left to my own devices, hanging by my hands over space, with the rope no longer any help to me.

A shiver ran down my spine. With great difficulty I got back to the right-hand side of the flake, succeeded in wedging myself in and got the rappel rope in position again. The platform

looked increasingly inaccessible, so we changed our tactics. I
went back to the right of the flake again, on to a minute ledge
a foot or so square, and there Boccalatte joined me, roping
down. We untied the two 100-foot ropes and roped up on one
of them. I went back to the flake and fixed a rope loop on to
it through which I threaded our second rope. Safeguarded in
this way I set off again on the slanting traverse. I progressed
for a few yards until I got close to a narrow ledge some four
inches wide. I warned Boccalatte to be ready for any contin-
gency. Reaching out with my left hand I got hold of the ledge,
let go the rappel and swung out into space. As my body
described a half-circle, my right hand got a hold as well, and
with a desperate effort I managed to pull myself up, and
knocked in a piton above me for a belay. The traverse was
finished.

We let ourselves down on the rope for another ten feet and
so came to the platform. Boccalatte went ahead, and in two
rope-lengths we reached the shoulder where we could bivouac.
It was then 7.30, and to make use of the remaining hour of
daylight we decided to climb another pitch and leave a rope
in position ready for the next day. While watching my rope out
of the corner of his eye Gabriele set about clearing the shoulder
of snow and stones, but I found myself seriously involved, so
much so in fact that I was obliged to ask Boccalatte to come up
beneath me to belay me. It took me a good forty minutes to
climb to the full length of the rope; then I roped down, back to
the ledge. We finished making preparations for the bivouac
and got out the tent.

There was not a cloud in the sky and the stars were already
looking down on us as we sat back to back in the narrow space
available and prepared for that long, familiar minute-counting
vigil. It was not cold, but round midnight a strong wind got
up and threatened to tear our silken shelter to shreds. Whenever I dozed off something very odd seemed to be happening.
I thought I was at sea, giving advice to a friend: "Nicholas, the
sail! Don't slack the sheet!" Then I woke to the flapping of
the tent, loud as a machine-gun. In the morning it was still
blowing, and we didn't dare venture out until the sun reached

us. Then, at 8.30, the wind stopped as if by magic, and at
9 o'clock we were ready to continue the ascent. But the wind
had played us a dirty trick: it had blown the rope we had left
hanging round the other side of the ridge, and we lost half an
hour before we succeeded in getting hold of the end. We then
hauled ourselves hand over hand up to the piton, and afterwards
continued more easily on the left of the ridge.

We were on the summit at 11 o'clock and stopped there for
half an hour. A rappel took us down to the slopes of the
Aiguille Blanche and, unroped, we sped down the ordinary
Peuterey route. In three hours we were back at our starting-
point, and another three hours took us down to the Gamba hut.
So ended the ascent of one of the most beautiful and most
difficult pure rock climbs of the Western Alps.

Eleven : 1939 to 1942

First ascent of the Piliers de Fresney route on Mont Blanc—Two attempts and first ascent of the east wall of the Grandes Jorasses

WHEN climbing in the Mont Blanc massif, I was often in the Val Ferret, sometimes for climbs in the Fréboudzie or Triolet basins, sometimes simply to enjoy the incomparable view of Mont Blanc which you get from the high pastures of this valley. How marvellous it looks when the sun sinks behind the wild Peuterey ridge and the last rays stab the sky and dissolve into the whiteness of the clouds, touching the Aiguille Noire with gold.

But if I went beyond Planpincieux, a green oasis frequented by well-to-do mountain-lovers, and continued past la Vachey, half-way between that hamlet and Sagioan, another vision drew my gaze, appearing suddenly at the far end of the Fréboudzie basin. At first I had been happy simply to admire this new aspect of the Grandes Jorasses—a mountain with such a splendid climbing history. Then the great triangular wall, rising above a strangely contorted glacier seamed with enormous crevasses, began to interest me for its own sake.

Would it be climbed one day? A first cursory examination suggested it wouldn't. Seen from a distance, and even when studied through powerful glasses, the upper part of the wall appeared like a gigantic slab of reddish, compact granite; here and there a few wrinkles and a few cracks showed up in certain lights and, after a fall of snow, a few white patches remained clinging to the walls. But there were other problems challenging us in other places, and for the moment the east wall of the Grandes Jorasses remained a distant and problematical ambition—a fruit both coveted and forbidden. There were many people who would have dearly liked to climb it yet were content to postpone their attempt, secure in the knowledge that its forbidding appearance would be defence enough for a long time to come.

In 1935, after the fall of the north face of the Grandes Jorasses, Gugliermina sent a postcard of the east face to Chabod and myself with a possible route marked and a friendly suggestion: "What about the east face?" A pleasant idea indeed; but the realisation of it was to be put off for some time. A few days later, while climbing the Hirondelles ridge, I was able to see the huge, terrifying slabs at close quarters, and I was anything but encouraged by what I saw.

Two more years were to pass before a serious attempt was really put in hand. In 1937 I went up to the Fréboudzie bivouac-shelter with Leo Dubosc, determined to go close enough to see whether the defences presented some vulnerable point at which they might be forced. But our attempt on the wall became an attempt merely to reach the foot of it, for we had the unfortunate notion of going straight up the true right-hand branch of the glacier and were unable to get through on account of the many unbridged crevasses. We were obliged to retreat after having circled round for nearly ten hours without even reaching the slope at the foot of the wall. However we had seen that we should have to go by way of the Col des Hirondelles; but next day it snowed. So we returned to Turin, without the pleasure of so much as setting foot on the lowest rocks.

In 1938 and 1939 my Alpine activity was rather curtailed by professional duties, but in 1940 I was called up to serve on the western front, and I found myself back at Courmayeur. Once hostilities with France were over and our unit had returned to its base at Courmayeur, I obtained leave to do some climbing from Captain Inaudi, who was commanding the unit and was a member of the Italian Academic Alpine Club. With the guide, Pennard, who was also in the army, I repeated the ascent of the south ridge of the Aiguille Noire de Peuterey. Then, as the weather was still fine and Paolo Bollini had come to Courmayeur, we succeeded in making the first ascent of the Piliers de Fresney route on Mont Blanc.

This route up Mont Blanc is interesting in itself, but it had

a quite special interest for me. Every time I had been in Courmayeur or Chamonix since 1931, some kind lady would enquire
about my Alpine adventures; then, having tried in vain to make
me describe "the most dramatic moment" of my ascents, and
having herself described with a wealth of detail the ascent which
some near relative of hers had made of the culminating point
of Mont Blanc, she would put the routine question with tremendous seriousness: "And how many times have *you* been to
the summit of Mont Blanc?" This question always put me in a
very awkward position. For if the truth were told, I should have
to admit that I had never been to the summit of Mont Blanc
at all. But how could I inflict such disillusionment upon my
amiable questioner? It would have put an abrupt end to her
admiration of my Alpine achievements! "What! You've never
been to the top of Mont Blanc? But even my niece has been
up!" So I used to content myself with some noncommittal
comment, "Ah yes, just so!" and at once turn the conversation
before compromising myself. But sooner or later I should have
to fill in such a serious omission.

The problem lay in the choice of a route, for there are many
ways leading direct to the summit of Mont Blanc, even leaving
aside the secondary routes, and the combinations with routes
up lesser peaks, and there is no lack of classic approaches.
Among the latter, the most important in order of difficulty,
according to Graham Brown and Alexander Graven, are: the
Pear, the Innominata ridge by the direct variation, the two
Sentinelle Rouge routes and the Peuterey ridge. In beauty, and
in distinction of character, there is nothing to choose between
these routes. Any mountaineer might well aim to climb them
all. But so far I had always put off doing any of them, for I
considered these ascents as special treats which I would taste in
the years to come, when I had finished with climbs of extreme
difficulty and could allow myself to enjoy, at leisure, and in a
due spirit of devotion, the whole series of great classic climbs.
But in the meantime I had to climb Mont Blanc.

Often, coming up from Pré-Saint-Didier, I had noticed that
in the curve of the great wall, between the Peuterey and
Innominata ridges, there stood out three gigantic red columns

of the finest granite imaginable, which I called the "pillars".
This wall, vast even by Mont Blanc standards, was still virgin,
and the ideal route would be up one of the pillars—the one
nearest the summit. But I had always been deterred by the
difficulties and length of the approach. In 1938, during the
ascent of the Picco Gugliermina with Gabriele Boccalatte, I
had examined the problem afresh. I knew, too, that there was
a possibility of a bivouac shelter being established on the Pointe
Eccles at about 13,000 feet, which would partly solve the
problem of the approach.

At last, in August 1940, the climb was ripe. Its happy
accomplishment, as well as giving us the pleasure of having
made our own route up Mont Blanc, left us a wealth of impressions and memories: the long traverse to the foot of the climb
along the base of the wall of the Pointe Eccles, on steep slopes
swept by avalanches; the difficult climbing on red granite in
the middle section of the pillar; the pitches of mixed rock and
ice when the axe, pulled from the sack, comes into play and
intensifies the impression of a hand-to-hand struggle; the final
treacherous little ridge beneath the séracs which we forced by
night in the uncertain shadow of the Brouillard arête; finally
the triumphant exit above the séracs in the brilliant light of a
full moon among whorls of snow blown up by a stormy north
wind; and then the summit, reached at midnight in an atmosphere beyond all imagining. A matchless harmony, a crescendo of stirring themes and variations such as no composer,
not even a Wagner, could describe or evoke.

After spending the rest of the night at the Vallot hut, we
went down to Courmayeur, physically and mentally ready for
the great battle for the east face of the Jorasses.

When we reached the Fréboudzie bivouac-shelter, the
weather seemed definitely favourable and we were resolved, if
necessary, to remain three days on the wall in order to get up.
But it is well known that decisions taken at the hut after a good
meal, and under the influence of a perfect sunset—as stimu-
lating to the senses as a heroic symphony—are often reversed
when the heavy, implacable shadow of the mountain weighs

down upon one with all its static force: we were once again to prove this true.

At 11 p.m. two climbers, Pittatore and Galeazzi, returned to the bivouac-shelter after doing the Rivero-Castelli route on the south arête of the Petites Jorasses. With a fine sense of camaraderie, they settled themselves temporarily outside, so as not to disturb us until, at 1 a.m., we set off and left the place to them.

We had the moon for our night march, and there was no need of a lantern as we threaded our way, very much by guesswork, between enormous crevasses in the shadow of the séracs, which glittered strangely in the starlight. We went slowly, and lost a bit of time in the last part by taking to the rocks on the right instead of climbing straight up to the col. We traversed across steep slopes on a level with the foot of the wall, with the intention of climbing direct to the large snow ledge and then bearing diagonally left, in order to reach a vertical dièdre which we thought would take us past the area of slabs. On the first part of the climb we moved rapidly, without encountering any particular difficulties, but when we came out on to the ledge, the sight of the great red overhanging slabs above rather damped our ardour. Paolo was curt: "Nothing doing." And in fact we searched in vain for a reasonable chance of forcing a way up the great wall. Even if we had succeeded in getting past the slabs, there appeared to be a line of overhangs across the whole wall forbidding further ascent. It remained to go up and make sure. Following the slanting line of broken rock leading to the dièdre, we met with the first difficulties in the shape of two little overhangs.

At 11 o'clock we reached a large terrace at the start of the dièdre. At a first cursory inspection it looked extremely difficult, but possible, although the roof above it made the exit problematical. I hoped to be able to traverse to the right before the top and to get into a depression which ran beneath the line of overhangs, and formed the only line of weakness in the centre of the wall. With this intention I moved determinedly to the attack on the left. It was very hard to begin with, and I had to use a few pitons in order to get up. Then, holding on to the rope, I traversed into the corner of the dièdre and continued pitoning up a narrow crack. After sixty feet I found a stance for my feet, stopped and brought up Paolo who had to make a daring swing on the rope to get to the little crack. He took my place at the pitons and I went on again. But as I got higher all hope of a way out vanished. The right-hand wall of the dièdre, which I had counted on traversing higher up in order to escape, was overhanging, and its smooth surface offered not the least crack. It would certainly have been possible to go on up to the top of the dièdre, but the roof above stuck out for several yards and was insurmountable. I went on for another thirty feet and then, realising the uselessness of my effort, came down again, leaving a karabiner in the last piton.

From the stance at which Paolo had joined me we roped down to the terrace. It was 1 o'clock, the sun had just disappeared behind the Tronchey arête and the temperature immediately dropped several degrees. Now we had to try to force a way to the central part of the wall at some other point. Paolo pointed out a vertical crack rising from the extreme right of the terrace, and insisted that I should climb it. Only twenty-five or thirty feet were visible, and after that one guessed that the wall fell back. Did the key to the climb lie beyond this crack? The twenty-five or thirty feet were certainly very difficult, but to climb up, and then probably come down again, would take only thirty to forty minutes. Clearly we ought to go up and see if we could discover anything further, but I stayed where I was in an agony of indecision. The south-west wind was blowing insistently, vast cirrus formations were massing over by the Col de la Seigne, and small dense clouds were beginning to appear between the lesser summits—all this made me very doubtful. To proceed further with the search for a possible route might perhaps mean getting caught by bad weather in the middle of the slabs. To delay our retreat might mean a disagreeable forced bivouac at the foot of the wall. The unshakeable determination that shapes events was now undermined by reason. I shivered, but not with cold—it was the feeling of a heavy shadow now beginning to get the upper hand, the awareness of those icy slabs never touched by the sun, of frozen tongues of ice on the overhangs. I decided on retreat, and Paolo agreed unwillingly for, as he used to put it, he could still feel "the lions roaring inside him".

In three rappels we dropped straight down to the large snow-ledge, from which we continued the descent more slowly. Our only consolation was that the sky was becoming increasingly overcast, but soon our annoyance at having had to give up a climb was swamped by our anxiety to avoid a bivouac on the descent. Owing to the sun's having disappeared long since behind the Tronchey ridge, the traverse from the foot of the wall across to the col was not very dangerous, but even so a few stones went whistling through the air. In fact one enormous block, which must have weighed at least a ton, and which was flat and triangular with sharp edges, gave us a most unusual sight: it fell like a thunder-bolt on to the snow slope, and shot down it at high speed, cutting through the soft snow like a speed-boat and throwing up two high sprays like a pair of frothy moustaches.

We did not stop at the col, for time pressed, but sped on down the long slopes in glissades, boldly taking the big crevasses in our stride. We managed to get clear of them just as the light was fading, and it was pitch dark on the moraine. However, I knew the ground well enough to make my way so accurately that we didn't realise we had arrived until we actually bumped into the bivouac-shelter, to the great astonishment of Paolo, who was accustomed to seeing me always go astray on well-known and well-marked paths.

In the morning, when we finally decided to get up, the clouds were already beginning to clear and great patches of blue appeared above the summits, but it had snowed heavily, quite low down. This sight cheered us up a bit and we decided that in the long run it is always best to follow one's judgment. Had we continued, who knows how it would have ended? This put a stop to any last recriminations, and we got ready to go down to Courmayeur. The expedition was now postponed for another year.

In 1941, after we had spent a week in the Brenta group to

complete our training, Paolo fell victim to a grave attack of doubt, and went off to Portofino. I knew Portofino only from hearsay, and I quite understood that it must be far more agreeable to relax in the calm waters of the Tyrrhenian Sea than to toil up peaks and glaciers; but I was beginning to think that a personal link was being forged between this Eden and myself, for this was the third time I had met it in my path. I foresaw that some day I too should have to go and find out what mysterious spell lay hidden behind the pines one caught sight of from the train. This was why I eventually went alone up the Aosta valley, after having arranged with Gagliardone that I would telegraph for him to come as soon as the weather was favourable. But the season was not propitious, and after waiting in vain for a week I returned to Turin.

Another year of waiting went by: then 1942 began most auspiciously. Returning from the Dolomites, I stopped for a week in Turin to attend to urgent business, then on August 8 I left for Courmayeur with Gagliardone. To my great regret Paolo was unable to join us this time; on his return from the Dolomites his military duties kept him in Turin and he did not know when he would be able to get off.

About 6 o'clock the same day we reached la Vachey, which we had decided to use as a base for operations. The weather was superb, and so also were conditions on the mountains. We held a brief council of war to draw up our programme. After having considered two or three plans of action we decided to leave next morning for the Col des Hirondelles in order to see what state the glacier was in that season—for we should have to go over it at night, without a moon—and also to leave a rucksack with ropes and heavy equipment at the col. This in fact was what we did, only, when we were half-way up the glacier, before we came to the area of big crevasses, we were tempted by the magnificent weather and decided to cut things short and attack the next day. We left the rucksack with the equipment in a filled-in crevasse, and went back to the bivouac-shelter. Gagliardone stayed there while I went down to la Vachey to fetch provisions for the climb; by 9 p.m. I was up again at Fréboudzie. The guide Arturo Ottoz, and Guido

Alberto Rivetti's eldest son with his friend Olcese, kept us company in the tiny shelter.

Next morning we left at 3.20. It was pitch dark and we made our way with difficulty over the boulders of the moraine, thinking of the delightful starts during our recent trip to the Dolomites, when we never set the alarm earlier than 7! The going was easier on the glacier in the uncertain light of the stars, but when we came to where we had to pick up the sack it was still dark and, as we might have foreseen, the sack could not be found. It may sound odd that, having left an object at a specific point, we were unable to find it. We both swore that it was the place all right, that we couldn't have made a mistake, but of the sack there was no trace. We began to wonder if the glacier had not played us a trick; then, to settle the matter I decided to go down a bit and pick up our previous day's tracks, and in this way I found the hole. Meanwhile an hour had gone by, and dawn was breaking. We went on up, feeling a bit chilled, and to save time we decided not to rope. But in the middle section of the glacier there were no longer the same through-routes as in previous years, and we were forced to make a wide détour to the left, going round some enormous crevasses. Time was flying and when we reached the col it was 8.30. We roped, and began the traverse leading to the start of the climb. However, under the couloir forming the leg of the Y whose two wide-angled arms form the large snow-ledge, we were obliged to stop; it was very dangerous here, for a continual hail of stones and icicles was coming down from the top of the wall, which had already been in the sun for a couple of hours. We remained where we were for half an hour, uncertain what to do, then, abandoning the place we had started from the two previous years, we tried to join the route higher up, crossing the couloir beneath an overhang. Water trickled down it, but it protected us sufficiently from the missiles. Though we carried on, we had lost so much time that when we got back on to the route, distinctly damp from our forced douche, we were four hours behind our 1940 times. When we reached the large terrace beneath the dièdre it was 3.30.

My anxiety to see what lay beyond the vertical crack made

me oblivious to all our misadventures, and, leaving my sack, I started up straight away. The crack was very hard, but I climbed it in one spurt with the help of a piton half-way up, and it brought me out on to a smaller terrace, where I had the extensive area of slabs before me. It looked as if I could continue easily and I called to Gagliardone to hurry up and tie on the sacks, which I then pulled up one at a time. This manœuvre had to be repeated at each pitch, for our sacks were extremely well stocked and the addition of crampons and ice-axes made them very heavy indeed. It meant a considerable expenditure of energy for me as well as a substantial loss of time, but it was essential. As soon as my friend joined me, I tackled the slab on the right. My illusions were short-lived. I climbed up another couple of yards, and then the holds became microscopic and I could only find closed cracks. I came down a little and went further to the left, succeeded in driving a piton less than an inch into the rock, continued my traverse with extreme difficulty and finally succeeded in reaching a dièdre split in the corner by a crack. I might just as well have started straight up on the left, but I should know better next time. After a few more yards of exceedingly difficult climbing, the angle lessened and I was able to continue comfortably. The forbidden door giving access to the central section of the wall had been broken open; it remained to be seen whether the exit would be forced as quickly. Another rope-length brought us to a terrace cutting right across the wall, much smaller than the one at the foot of the great dièdre and tilted outwards; we could return to it if we found no bivouac site higher up. Above the terrace the wall overhung, but on the right there was another vertical dièdre. This succession of dièdres and terraces is one of the characteristics of the face and it is this alone that allows the climber to zigzag his way between the overhanging slabs. I climbed up at the back of it, putting in three pitons; then, when the crack widened, I succeeded with great difficulty in getting out on to the right-hand wall where I managed to get a piton into a circular hole which solved the problem. Gagliardone hauled on the two ropes from as directly underneath as possible; I collected myself for the effort, then I called to him to let the ropes run slack, and at the same instant I launched myself out and came to a stance. I pulled the sacks up, and Gagliardone joined me. The dièdre still ran up, overhanging, and I kept on up the back as far as a belay on two pitons where it was very difficult to change places. To haul up the sacks I had to resort to a complicated manœuvre: first I pulled one of the ropes up as usual to free it from the karabiners, then I had to throw it down again to Gagliardone, but on account of the overhang the rope hung too far out and I was obliged to repeat the attempt five times. However, things went better with the second sack—an old hand now, I was successful at the second throw.

Meanwhile the evening shadows had filled the valleys and the moment was approaching when we should have to stop. Thirty feet higher up there appeared to be an inviting terrace, but when I reached it, it proved to be a slab only slightly less tilted than the rest. The only place where we could stop at all comfortably was the little terrace 130 feet below. I told Gagliardone to belay himself to a piton with some line and then unrope, so that I could arrange the rappel to go down. The two hundred-foot ropes just reached the stance above the terrace, but the slanting overhang of the dièdre pushed them out. We should have to swing in to the wall. Gagliardone went down and belayed himself, then it was my turn. Naturally when we tried to pull the rope down afterwards from underneath the overhang, it wouldn't run through the rappel loop. This put us in an awkward predicament. It seems incredible, but on almost all the climbs I have done with difficult rappels, at least once I have had trouble with the rope getting jammed. It happened on the Cima de Gasperi, the south side of the Pic Adolphe Rey, the north face of the Grandes Jorasses, and on many other occasions. The fault was largely due to carelessness, but chance must have had a hand in it too. This time the moment was decidedly ill-chosen, for it was nearly 9 o'clock and there was not much daylight left. After the usual unsuccessful attempts, there was nothing for it but the usual solution: to climb up the rope hand over hand, while oneself unroped, at least as far as the belay pitons where we had changed places. The manœuvre was far from simple and very

risky, for when I hung on the rope it swung me out away from
the rock into space. On my first attempt I tried to keep in the
corner of the dièdre, only partly using the rope. I succeeded in
getting up fifteen feet or so and then gave up and came down.
Having to trust oneself, without any safeguard, simply to the
strength of one's hands gripped round a rope too thin to give
a good hold, is really far too disagreeable a sensation. But the
situation in which we found ourselves did not admit of many
solutions. It was impossible to climb unaided down the thirty
feet separating us from the bivouac site; consequently either we
had to bivouac standing up on the restricted space where we
now perched, or else manage to retrieve the rope. Darkness
began to engulf the wall and everything else, there was no time
to study the alternatives, and I just had to decide to take the
risk. I seized the rope in both hands and hauled myself up as
quickly as possible with my feet stretching towards the right-
hand wall, smooth and distant, in whose direction the pull of
the rope was taking me. Twenty, twenty-five, thirty feet . . .
As I went higher I came nearer to the wall. At last I managed
to get my feet on to two holds. I still had six feet to go before
reaching the stance, and I began to get cramp in my arms and
hands from the violent effort required of already much tried
muscles. Another yard . . . another rest . . . Then keeping my
balance by holding the rope in my teeth, I managed to grab a
large hold with my free left hand and to reach the pitons at the
stance. From this position I succeeded in getting the rope to
run, passed it through one of the pitons, and roped down
rapidly. Gagliardone was pleased but unperturbed for, partly
due to the darkness and partly to his position, he had been
unaware of the tense moment of drama I had been through.
But it was over quickly and the instant, only a few seconds
ago, when I might have lost my life, already seemed remote.

It was dark by the time we were at last able to settle ourselves
on the terrace. A bivouac, as everyone knows, is a test of
patience which one does one's best to curtail by taking as long
as one possibly can over the preliminaries. But once installed
in the little tent, after one has leisurely eaten a few provisions,
changed socks and done a hundred other little jobs, then if one

dares risk a glance at the time it is sure to be no later than
11 p.m. And for the whole of the rest of the night there remains
only the usual unsatisfactory distraction of thinking about
things that contrast most with one's present position.

At the first hint of dawn we saw that the sky was overcast.
Low-lying mist covered the valley; the horizon was hidden
behind long banks of cloud. Even if the sun eventually succeeded in piercing the curtain of cirrus it would be very late
before we felt any warmth. Towards 8.30 the weather seemed
to improve and we started off. I repeated the pitch up the
doubled rope as far as the stance; then suddenly we were
enveloped in mist, and sleet began to patter against the rock.
We exchanged views at a distance, agreed that it would be
best not to push on, and I came down. But scarcely had we
regained the terrace when a gust of wind swept away the mist
and a ray of sunshine reappeared in the cloudy sky. The wind,
however, was still blowing from the west. We put off making a
decision until later, and thought we would wait a bit before
giving up. Around 10 o'clock the weather improved, and we
continued the climb. It was no longer possible to proceed
directly from the furthest point reached the evening before, so
we traversed along to the right over difficult ice formations in
order to reach a depression in the rock beneath the "Tower"—
a sort of rock spur to which I had given this name when
examining the climb through glasses. From where we were
now it looked entirely different, and all we could see was a
smooth overhanging wall rising above our heads. At first sight
there seemed to be three possibilities of forcing this wall: on the
left, a smooth vertical crack with sloping sides and quite without
holds; in the middle, a depression in the rock which would have
given some hope if it had not been thickly coated with verglas!
and on the right, where the spur stood out from the wall, a
kind of chimney-dièdre which in fact was hidden from view.
Rather disappointed by the look of what I could see, I decided
to try what I could not see. A large, smooth, and unclimbable
slab separated me from the chimney. However, at the point
where this slab met the wall of the tower, there were some
cracks into which one could get one's fingers and I climbed up

with extreme difficulty in a layback position. After fifty feet of
exceedingly hard climbing I rounded the ridge which formed
one side of the dièdre to face an unpleasant surprise: the exit of
the dièdre was barred by a thick tongue of green ice! I saw at
once that it was impossible, and came down on the rope—I had
run it through a karabiner attached to a piton, and both were
left behind—and joined Gagliardone. In the excitement of the
struggle we had scarcely noticed that the clouds had closed in
once more and that sleet had again begun to beat on our hoods.

It was 2 o'clock and we realised that things were not going
too well. We now had to choose, without further delay, between a second bivouac—not knowing where or how—and a
hasty retreat which might perhaps enable us to get back to
Fréboudzie before nightfall. As on the previous occasion I
could feel the mountain asserting itself suddenly and terrifyingly;
all our determination seemed to evaporate. There was nothing
for it but to go down.

Rapidly as spiders we dropped down the rappels, plunging
into the mist. Our object now was to reach the glacier far
below as quickly as possible. Now and again, it snowed. At
6.30 we were at the foot of the climb and at 7.15 we reached
the col. We made our way blindly, in dense mist, but managed
to come out on to the slope at exactly the right place. Our
hopes of reaching the shelter were dwindling, yet we kept on as
fast as we could. It was already nearly dark, and when we
came to the area of big crevasses we could not find the way we
had followed on the ascent. I forged ahead among the séracs
and had to climb down to the bottom of one enormous crevasse
and up again the other side. We were lucky, and by taking a
chance we managed to win through the ice-fall. We continued
on down easy slopes in the dark until we came to the other lot
of crevasses which separated us from the moraine, and there
things became more tricky. It was hard to distinguish between
the white of the glacier and the black gaping holes, and our
electric torches had given out. After groping our way round a
bit, we made a sensible decision. The way off was somewhere
within a fairly circumscribed area, bounded on the left by a
wall of séracs, and this area was seamed with large parallel

crevasses criss-crossed by other crevasses, forming a regular labyrinth. We knew that at the end of one of these ridges of ice running between two parallel crevasses, lay the one and only way off. But which of them all was the right one? As we couldn't tell in the dark, we went above the wall of séracs and began investigating each tongue of ice in an attempt to find the way by a process of elimination. The first we followed led us to enormous black holes which we guessed rather than saw; so we patiently retraced our steps and began again. At the seventh or eighth attempt, the ridge of ice narrowed and ran on down and up again without a break. We moved carefully forward, holding our axes in front of us like blind people with their sticks. Gradually the black spaces became smaller and fewer, and at last I was able to give the longed-for shout to Gagliardone, who was following some fifteen yards behind holding on to the rope in readiness for any emergency: "We've made it!" Our crampons drew sparks from the stones on the ice. This time, too, I let myself be guided by instinct and it was little more than midnight when I stumbled against the Fréboudzie bivouac-shelter.

In the morning we were wakened by a party from Turin who were camping in the barns of Tronchey. After yesterday's various threats of snow, the bad weather had stopped short and in the morning the sky was absolutely clear. But we had to give up for a while. Our hands were painful from contact with verglas and snow, and we were very weary, so down we went to la Vachey.

A few days went by, and badly as our bodies needed the rest, we could not find peace of mind. Our nerves were all on edge during this forced inactivity, and the tension mounted day by day, all the more so since both our attempts had left me still in doubt as to the possibility of continuing the route. Two major unknown factors remained to be resolved: the "Tower", and the final band of overhangs which might well halt us a few yards from our goal.

We left la Vachey after dinner on August 15 at 7.30 and this time started out in uncertain weather. Large clouds hung stationary in the sky all day, but towards evening the situation

improved. We reached Fréboudzie at 9 o'clock and after a
good sleep set out at 3 a.m. beneath a starry sky. We made
rapid progress and when we crossed the central portion of the
glacier it was still dark; by lanternlight we went down again
into the large crevasse, following our tracks of the week before.
We did not rope up this time and so were moving much more
quickly. At 6.30 we were on the col, and by 7.30 had reached
the foot of the climb. While we uncoiled the rope and had a
bite, a few icicles began to whistle through the air. At 8 o'clock
we started up. Three hours later we were on the terrace beneath the great dièdre, and here we stopped to eat again. The
pitons we had left further on were a great help. By 1 o'clock
we came to the little bivouac ledge, and at 2.30 the "Tower"—
the highest point we had reached seven days before—and now
we had to solve the major problem of getting up it. Of the
three ways which had previously appeared possible the only one
still untried was the furthest to the left—the narrow vertical
crack. From below I thought it would go all right, and I looked
forward to the delights of a sixty-foot pitch, extremely difficult
and strenuous, without any possibility of a belay, above a huge
drop; one of those pitches which, once one is safely up oneself,
make one think with pleasure of other climbers waiting their
turn to attempt it!

My enthusiasm was short-lived. As I mounted I felt the
smooth, rounded edges pushing me gently but irresistibly outwards, and after ten hard-won feet I had the distinct feeling
that in another eighteen inches I should be in mid-air. Indeed
it was already very questionable how I should get down. I
jammed one leg in as far as I could (these cracks did at least
have one advantage—one could remain in position for a certain
length of time) and, stretching out on to the right-hand wall, I
found a thin crevice in which I managed to insert a piton for
just over an inch. Then, held by the rope—though I didn't
have all my weight on it—I descended. But as I moved outwards I noticed that, at the start of the crack, in the overhanging wall, a slanting cleft ran up which was just right for
pitoning. I moved across towards it and drove in a piton
firmly. The way out at the top was overhanging, and beyond

only the sky was visible; but I had to go up as far as that, any-how, to see what happened. I made height gradually, using the ropes as pulleys. This time the pitch did not disappoint us; so the solution was none of the three possibilities we had envisaged, but a fourth. Above the "Tower" the angle of the rock fell back for three rope-lengths and then steepened again into a broad rampart of overhangs stretching right across the whole breadth of the wall. This was the final obstacle which, when seen from below, had caused us the greatest misgiving. It did in fact appear at first sight to be insurmountable, for the rock was compact, without any fissures. However, at one point, slightly over to the left, there was a dip in the girdle of overhangs and there the wall was no more than sixty feet high. Easy rocks brought us to this wall, which overhung noticeably, with a corbel of at least three feet. We found a small dièdre with a crack at the back which continued up for forty feet or so, and then splayed out at the top; it was impossible to say whether it would go above that point, so we just had to start up and trust to luck. The pitons held very well, and the main difficulty lay in the continuity and degree of effort required.

After an hour's work I reached the spot where the crack opened out, and I was then able to see another little crack which ran up obliquely; but this looked like petering out before the end of the overhang. I badly wanted to go down to rest for a bit, but I was forced on by my anxiety to see the final outcome of the pitch, and by the evening shadows which had already begun to envelop the mountains. Foot by foot I made my way up; it was very tiring. Then the crack petered out, but from the last piton I could reach up to the top of the wall with my hands just where there was a distinct dip in the rock. Right to the end we were haunted by the nightmare of an impassable pitch. I clawed at some minute rugosities—"Hold on still!—Ready? Slack off!"—and the minute I felt the ropes go slack I gave a violent thrust upwards, for not only had I to heave up the weight of my body, but I had also to reckon with the friction of the ropes running through a number of karabiners. However the holds were good, and soon I found myself on the slabs of the last great ledge which, when we had examined the climb through glasses, had seemed to indicate victory a hand's breadth away, and the prospect of a bivouac on comfortable terraces. But for the moment the terraces were much higher up on the right and I had to be content with a space between two slabs where I put in a couple of pitons to belay Gagliardone, and to which I fastened the sacks after pulling them up. This all took some time, and to husband my strength and save time, Gagliardone decided not to recover any of the pitons. At 8.30 we were together on the stance.

The sloping slabs that separated us from the terraces were not at all the easy matter we had supposed, and before long I found myself in difficulties again. I had to give up trying to climb them direct, and was obliged to skirt round them higher up where the rampart ended beneath another wall. So we made an ascending traverse, slanting to the right for two rope-lengths. We had already begun to savour the prospective delights of a peaceful and comfortable bivouac, with all anxiety behind us and the climb successfully in the bag, when we came to a place where water had been running down the rock; at this late hour it had become a thick layer of transparent ice. I tried it with my hammer; it was authentic verglas, frozen solid to the rock, and I realised straight away that there was little we could do about it. All the same I tried to climb up it, making use of a few rugosities which I first chipped out with the hammer, but two or three times I nearly slipped and so gave it up.

It was dark, and to move was dangerous. We had to resign ourselves to stopping a hundred feet short of the bivouac site we could see higher up—a regular esplanade between large blocks—and to settle down as best we could where we were. We had at our disposal a sloping scoop between two adjacent slabs—it was about twelve to sixteen inches wide and six feet long—where we could at least sit down; we belayed ourselves to pitons and put the tent over our heads. Between us we left a space of about eighteen inches where we could put the candle and light the meta stove to make tea, and, as we still had a flask full of water, we organised a regular service: at the odd hours we lit the candle for a quarter of an hour; at the even hours we made tea. In this way we were able to keep the cold

at bay; but the discomfort of our position and the impossibility
of moving soon weighed upon us. Summoning all the patience
I could command I succeeded in keeping quiet, but Gagliardone could not keep still, and wriggled this way and that. Our
position was indeed far from pleasant and as usual the hours
dragged by exasperatingly. But morning always comes.

We were stirred out of our torpor by the first rays of sun
warming up the air inside the tent. We got up, packed our
sacks, and did a few exercises to start up our circulation and
restore normal movement to our joints. At 8 o'clock I got ready
to tackle the verglas again, for it wouldn't have melted till at
least 10 o'clock. In daylight I soon found a way round: I
climbed up some yards on the left and put in a piton, then I
traversed across on the rope so as to get into the crack above
the ice, and so continued the climb. After this the difficulties
were really at an end. We followed a ledge of broken rock by
which we reached the junction of the Tronchey and Hirondelles ridges, and at 11 o'clock we were up. We stopped on a
large rock terrace, about twenty yards from the dome of ice
that forms the summit, and stretched ourselves out in the sun.
It was hot, and we badly wanted to sleep. We felt no shiver of
joy, no ecstasy in victory. We had reached our objective, and
already it lay behind us. A dream had become reality—and I
felt something close to bitterness. How much finer it would be,
I couldn't help thinking, to long for something all one's life, to
fight for it without respite, and never to achieve it!

But this was only another episode. Down in the valley again
I should at once look round for some other goal, and if it didn't
exist, I would create it! I do not know why people associate
a man's happiness with the satisfaction of all his desires—a kind
of eternal beatitude, which could just as well be a state of complete apathy. The completely happy man would have nothing
left to say, nothing left to do. For myself I prefer an unattain-
able happiness, always near, always elusive: the prize which
vanishes every time one grasps it, to give way to another,
still harder, still more distant. The moments when the heart
really overflows with happiness come when the sense of life is
heightened by tension and struggle—the actual moments of

conquest, or more often of defeat, and not the dead moments when victory has been achieved.

Sleepier and sleepier we felt in the sun's warmth, but we had to bestir ourselves and go down. It was slightly past midday when we began the descent; very slowly, taking our time, we moved down to the valley.

East wall of the Grandes Jorasses with the hut built as a
memorial to Gervasutti

On the east wall of the Grandes Jorasses

The East wall of the Grandes Jorasses with the Gervasutti route marked. The Walker Spur and the Hirondelles Ridge are on the right.

The North-east face of Mt. Blanc du Tacul. The Gervasutti
Pillar (named in memory of the climber) falls directly from
the summit, to the right of the narrow ice gully

Twelve : Conclusion

THE little train ambled along and at every curve I felt it might leave the rails and take a rest beneath the fir-trees; the ascent was too steep for its worn-out pistons, and it gasped and spluttered its way up the valley. Sitting in a corner of the practically empty coach, I turned over in my mind the impulses which had brought me to the hills, and I dreamed of climbs to come.

I had set out alone, as I often did that particular year. The popular view of solitary climbing is that it is simply a form of suicidal mania; and that the individual has no right to devote himself of his own free will to a sport involving such excessive risks. But it seemed to me that a solitary wanderer like Lammer[1] had found in mountaineering a practical application of his Nietzschean philosophy, and, urged on by his inner demon, climbed mountains in search of difficulties and dangers for their own sake. Or there was Preuss,[2] who went as a conqueror from summit to summit, from victory to victory, disdaining all means of protection, sometimes linking another climber to his destiny, more often alone—as he was when he won his most brilliant victory, as he was when, betrayed by a treacherous hold, he fell to his death. My aim was more modest than theirs: it was to lose, on the heights, all those evil humours accumulated during the long monotonous hours of city life; to find serenity and calm in the freedom and exhilaration of climbing on difficult rock, in the long silent communion with the sun, the wind, the blue sky, in the nostalgic sweetness of the sunset. And no softer or more passive view of life could make me change my mind. Such were my thoughts as the train puffed its way up.

I reached the little station in darkness. The storm which

---

[1] A fanatical Swiss climber who made a principle of undertaking long and difficult climbs alone.
[2] Paul Preuss was killed in 1913 on the Manndlkogel in the Dachstein. He was 27 at the time of his death and had climbed more than 1,200 summits. His most brilliant achievement was the ascent and descent, solo, of the east wall of the Guglia di Brenta. [*Translators' Notes.*]

had been raging throughout the journey had only just abated, water was still pouring off the houses and trees, and the paths were muddy streams. Above the blackness of the mountains, clouds scudded across the sky before a driving wind, and the stars were beginning to come out. I had never climbed here before, though I had once driven through the valley; as I wanted to reach the hut that same night I looked on the list of paths for the distinctive mark to follow. A boy passed by, so I asked him where the mule-track started up.

"Do you want to go up now?" he asked.

"Yes, I want to do a climb, and I have to be back tomorrow evening."

"The path isn't well-marked; it's difficult to follow in the woods, and there is no moon. It will be quite a business finding the hut."

"Never mind, I've got an electric torch, I can look for the marks."

"All right: at the last house you turn right. To begin with there is a decent-sized mule-track, then, on the edge of the wood, you will find the path."

"Thanks very much; goodbye!"

He looked a bit dubious and stopped a minute to watch while I started slowly up. After wandering for a while among the pines and on the higher pastures, taking twice the normal time, I knocked at the door of the hut at two in the morning, drank two steaming grogs, and then lay down fully dressed on one of the bunks to rest for a couple of hours.

I left the hut at dawn. As the slope grew steeper I made my way up lightly with the cool mountain air giving me that delicious sensation of floating. My body was tingling with a wonderful sense of well-being, and ready to rise to whatever demands I made on it.

The weather had not completely cleared: wisps of mist curled round the yellow towers, alternately masking and re-vealing them, ghostly, distant, higher and bolder than in real life. I climbed up a grassy ridge, treading on a staircase of tufts, then on scree, slithery and exhausting like all Dolomite scree, but short, and so came to the foot of the climb where I changed my nailed boots for espadrilles. I took the rope from my sack and slung it round me, but I had neither pitons nor hammer, for I knew that on the descent I should find rappel loops already in position. Leaving sack and boots under a boulder, I approached the rock.

It began by a not very difficult vertical crack. I touched the rock with my hand, almost stroking it, as one strokes something one loves but has not seen for some time. It was still cold, but when I looked up the sun—seen through the mist, a yellow disc with a halo round it—had already appeared above a jagged ridge. Everything round me was quiet, with the rather startled silence of high places. I rubbed my foot two or three times on a polished bit of rock, as though to test its adherence, then I raised my arms in search of holds for my hands and, bracing my muscles, began to climb. I moved very slowly, without the least hurry, quietly looking for holds, studying each move so as to economise effort to the full. When a climber is on his own he can't afford to make the slightest mistake, for if he does, there is neither rope nor piton to save him. If his nerve goes, there is no friend to encourage him. And if danger suddenly strikes, all he can do is to risk everything; but if he loses, it is his life that is forfeit.

All went well for about four hours, and the higher I climbed, the more impressive appeared the vertical wall beneath me. Down below, very far below, the last scattered fir-trees appeared as minute dots against the grassy ridge.

I had done about three-quarters of the climb, and was in a chimney blocked by an enormous chockstone which I had to get over. I went up with my legs wide apart, arrived beneath the chockstone, got round it by wriggling my body between it and the wall and then, raising my hands, I took hold of it. I now had to swing out under the overhang and mantelshelf up. Kicking off with my feet, I made the effort.

But I had miscalculated. My chin came only on a level with the edge and I looked about for other handholds, but higher up the chockstone was rounded, smooth and polished without the vestige of a crack. So I let myself down slowly, trying to get my feet back on to their holds, but as my face was right up against the rock, I could not see. Beneath the overhang was the chimney, dropping down into space. I tried in every direction; it was no good. Although my feet did come in contact with the rock, I couldn't find the holds. I realised then that if I did not get up at once, all was over: the drop to the scree was getting on for 1,000 feet. I gave a spring and pulled up again on my fingers, but I could not get beyond the point I'd already reached. A shiver ran down my spine. Again I made the effort, even using my teeth to get a hold, with no other result than a bloody mouth. I slipped back, still clinging with my finger-tips to the sloping edge, and stayed there, panting, for a few minutes; and while I tried unsuccessfully to find a reasonable way out of this fix, my strength began to ebb. My fingers were gradually slipping from the holds, and I could no longer see or think. Then, in a fury, I succeeded in giving a heave that brought my chest above the upper edge of the chockstone. For a fraction of a second I managed to hold myself in position with the help of my chin while I reversed one hand and got it palm downwards on the rock. I transferred my weight to it, holding on by friction, gradually pushed myself up and, with a final effort, got my body on to the chockstone and lay down, utterly exhausted. When the trembling caused by nervous reaction began to subside, I sat up and looked down into the valley. Everything was just as it had been before. In the stillness of the air there was nothing to give away my presence. The grey mountain was indifferent. The valley floor was green and peaceful. Even the wind had died down. It was I, and I alone, who had sought this moment of suspense, created it, compelled it. Everything round me was motionless and static, had played no active part. And again the question surged up: "Why?"

No answer came—perhaps it never would. But when I reached the sun-flooded summit, with waves of floating mist beneath me, my heart sang for joy. The exaltation of that moment, out of the world, on the glory of the heights, would be justification enough for any rashness.

Reading through these lines, written many years ago about

a venture of my younger days, I have often asked myself the same question: "Why?" And I know now how impossibly difficult it would be to give any clear answer.

There are many people more competent than myself, at any rate in the art of writing, who have tried to give an answer, without much result beyond the controversies they have stimulated. I find it entirely natural that such attempts to define mountaineering should have produced no satisfactory result. For there is no such thing as objective mountaineering, there is only a form of activity, generically termed mountaineering, which enables certain people to express themselves, or gives them a means of satisfying an inner need, just as there are other forms of activity and other means by which other people may try to attain the same ends.

Of course, since the need is completely different for each individual, we have many forms of mountaineering. It may take the form of a need to live heroically, or to rebel against restraint and limitation: an escape from the restricting circle of daily life, a protest against being submerged in universal drabness, an affirmation of the freedom of the spirit in dangerous and splendid adventure. Or it may well be the pleasure of feeling strong and fit: of realising, in one controlled harmony, physical fitness and moral energy, elegance of style and calculated daring; ordeals gaily faced with friends themselves as firm as rock, the hard life of the high huts, the happy relaxation on remote pastures as one smokes a pipe or sings mountain songs. It may be the search for an intense aesthetic experience, for exquisite sensations, or for man's never satisfied desire for unknown country to explore, new paths to make. Best of all, it should be all these things together.

It follows that, at a certain moment one's personal preference for a particular line is bound to lead to the formation of a set of values. When a man, rising above the banality of his everyday existence, tries in one way or another to create for himself a higher mode of life, there are generally two possibilities open to him: either the way of pure imagination, or some mode which can be transformed into reality through action.

The first is generally considered the superior; but to be able to endow pure thought with a value, one must be a poet and an artist. Only those who have attained to poetry can allow themselves the luxury of giving a universal value to the creations of their imagination, while remaining comfortably in their armchairs. But the others, and among them mountaineers, if they do not wish to limit themselves to the pleasures of imagination, must seek the satisfaction of their spirit's needs in action, and this satisfaction will be greater, and more complete, in proportion to the intensity of the action.

In other words it seems to me that the contemplative side of mountaineering can only have an interpretative value, and that the ecstasy of creation can come from action alone.

But over and above all these academic analyses, one fact remains: the battle one fights on the mountain for hours on end, when life hangs by a thread above dizzy precipices, as one forces a route up the cold rock, or cuts an icy staircase to the sky, is work fit for men. Rocks that rise in a wondrous architecture, ice-couloirs that climb to the sky, the sky itself—always the same, yet endlessly varied, sometimes a deep blue in which the soul melts and merges with the infinite, sometimes streaked with storm clouds that weigh like lead upon the spirit—what unforgettable moments our mountains give us!

To the young climber facing the harsh ordeals of the Alps for the first time, I would recall the words of a friend who fell on a great mountain: "Dare all, and you will be kin to the gods."

GLOSSARY

arête, ridge, generally one of the main ridges of a mountain.

arriero, muleteer.

artificial climbing, climbing with the aid of pitons, étriers and tension (*q.v.*).

belay, to secure the climber to a projection with the rope; the projection itself.

bergschrund, a large crevasse separating the upper slopes of a glacier from the steeper ice or rock above.

chimney, a narrow vertical gully or fissure in rock or ice.

cirque, enclosing amphitheatre of mountains.

col, pass.

cornice, overhanging mass of snow or ice along a ridge, shaped like the curling crest of a wave and formed by the prevailing wind.

couloir, gully or furrow in a mountain side; may be of rock, ice or snow.

crampon, metal frame with spikes, fitting the soles of the boots, for use on hard snow or ice.

crevasse, a fissure in a glacier, often of great depth.

cwm, hanging valley scooped out of a mountain side.

dièdre, used to describe a pitch where two vertical planes of rock meet and form a wide-angled or "open" corner or groove; frequently there is a crack running up in the angle.

demi-lune, literally crescent moon : descriptive term applied to any crescent-shaped feature.

direttissima, a route up a mountain keeping to a direct line with no deviations.

étrier, a rope stirrup, usually with three rungs of light metal, which is clipped on to a piton and in which the climber stands.

espadrilles, rope-soled canvas boots.

gendarme, rock tower or tooth on a ridge.

ice-fall, a much torn and crevassed portion of a glacier caused by a change of angle or direction in the slope.

karabiner, large metal spring-loaded clip, which can be fixed to the rope or to a piton.

layback, method of climbing using a sideways pull on vertical holds with the feet braced against the wall.

line, a thin rope used for rappel or roping down (*q.v.*).

mantelshelf, method of getting on to a ledge above, by an armpull up which is then converted to a press down.

marteau-piolet, a piton-hammer with a rather long handle and a small pick for use on ice or snow.

moraine, long ridge or bank of stones and débris carried down by a glacier.

névé, upper snows which feed the glaciers; patch of old hardened snow, usually above the permanent snow line.

penitentes, ice-pinnacles, sometimes seven or eight feet high, found on Andean and Himalayan glaciers and formed by the action of the sun.

pitch, section of difficult ice or rock, anything from 10 to 120 feet in length, where climbers usually move one at a time.

piton, metal spike with a hole in the head which can be driven into crevices or cracks in the rock; a long thin type is used for ice.

Prusik loop, loop of line or thinnish cord which is doubled round the main climbing rope in such a way that with a downward pull it tightens up and does not slip. When no weight is applied it can be pushed up. With two such loops (plus an extra loop round the body for comfort) a climber can climb up a rope by which he is suspended, standing first in one loop while he pushes the other one up, and so on.

rappel or rope down, system of descending steep pitches by means of a rope doubled round a projection. Usually the thin rope known as line is used.

rognon, large hummock of rock protruding through a glacier.

rope, attaches members of a party together; a party may be referred to as a "rope".

scarpetti, *see* espadrilles.

scree, slope of small loose stones.

sérac, tower or pinnacle of ice, found mainly in ice-falls.

snow-bridge, a layer of snow bridging a crevasse.

spigolo, near-vertical rock ridge.

spur, rib of rock.

tension climbing, involves the leader being held in position by the alternate use of two ropes used as pulleys running from his waist up to and through a karabiner clipped to a piton above and then down to the second below who maintains tension as required.

traverse, to move horizontally across a mountain slope or face; to cross a mountain from one side to another.

verglas, thin coating of ice on rock.

vibrams, boots with heavy cleated rubber soles first made in Italy: the name derives from Vitale Bramani, one of the inventors.

Approximate British equivalents of continental grading of *rock pitches*:

Grade III	Difficult to easy Very Difficult.
Grade IV	Very Difficult to Mild Severe.
Grade V	Severe to easy Very Severe.
Grade VI	Very Severe.